Table of Contents

CHAPTER ONE

Introduction

I find it a bit ironic to want to author a book without really understanding who the audience is. When I wrote my first book, *Unfair Lending*, in 2022, I wanted to share my thoughts with both the banking industry and the everyday consumer. My goal was to educate lending organizations on how to build a stronger fair lending program, but at the same time, I hoped anyone could pick it up and learn more about the lending industry.

While some consumers did read it, overwhelmingly, it was bankers who became the main audience. I suppose it was a banking book after all. Since so many bankers found value in that first book, this one is specifically written for you. That means we are going much deeper into many of the key concepts I first covered in *Unfair Lending*.

~ Tory Haggerty

FAIR LENDING IS NOT ROCKET SCIENCE

Fair lending is often presented as an overly complicated topic. We are led to believe it is too difficult to figure out, and that you need to understand statistics, software, and regression analyses before you can even begin. Most fair lending training is an hour-long session where someone recites definitions, highlights a few hot topics, and then gives a couple of examples of how other organizations messed up. How is that helpful?

We, on the other hand, do not think fair lending is all that difficult. At its core, it is a matter of simple concepts, thoughts, and ideas that, when put together, create a framework for making loans the right way. If you stick with us until the end, we will show you. Yes, there are complicated concepts, but none of this is rocket science. If our Midwest public school education helped us figure this stuff out, we know you can do it too.

WHO WE ARE

Tory brought along a friend on this third book's journey. Jon Gilmor helped co-write this book. Like Tory, Jon is also a commissioned examiner with the FDIC with years of experience in both consumer compliance and specifically in fair lending. Most of the stories throughout this book will be from our combined perspective and experience.

Tory owns an audit company that performs dozens of fair lending audits every year. In fact, Tory has participated in more than 600 bank audits and Jon has participated in hundreds of his own. That means we have seen some wild stuff. We have seen a lot of great ways of doing things, and we have seen a lot of crazy ways of doing things. We are going to share those stories with you over the course of this book.

Stories help simplify complicated issues, but ultimately, the goal is to stop problems from happening in the first place. It is almost never better to fix a problem after the fact than it is to prevent it from even happening in the first place. We believe fair lending is no exception to that rule. Institutions pay millions to clean up fair lending issues and suffer reputational damage that can linger for years. Prevention is not only easier and cheaper, but it is also the right and smart thing to do.

WHY WE WRITE

We attend a lot of banking compliance conferences, and we have handed out thousands of copies of *Unfair Lending* along with Tory's second book, *Thick Red Line*. Our mission is to end illegal discrimination in lending, and to do that, we believe as many people as possible need to understand how fair lending should truly work.

When Tory returned to some of these same conferences year after year, attendees that received copies of *Unfair Lending* came up to him to thank him personally. One person even said they learned *everything* they knew about fair lending from reading his first book. While that might sound flattering, it is actually pretty scary. If compliance professionals who have been in the industry for 15 or 20 years claim that everything they know about fair lending is from a few hours with a free book they picked up from a conference, that tells you how badly more education is needed.

The goal of *Unfair Lending* was to teach how to build prevention into fair lending programs. For years, we sat through fair lending training where the focus was always on the past: case studies of how others failed. Do not get us wrong – case studies are valuable and can be a great way to take complex issues and make them relatable to everyday situations. There were plenty of stories in *Unfair Lending*, and readers found them valuable. We plan to tell even more stories in this book because stories are one of the easiest and most interesting ways to learn. We also want to change the focus to the future. Fair lending issues are much easier to prevent than fix after the fact.

WHO THIS BOOK IS FOR

In this book, we will cover the basics of the loan life cycle, similar to *Unfair Lending*, but with much greater depth. Tory learned after writing *Unfair Lending* that the true audience of these books are bankers: specifically, compliance and audit professionals working inside the industry. However, loan officers, executives, and other key decision makers within financial institutions are also our target audience. If you work in lending, in any capacity, you are in the right place.

If that is you, we want you to walk away with a clearer picture of how things can go wrong and how to set things up for success. We will look at horror stories of institutions that failed, not to point fingers, but to use them as learning tools.

Since 2019, Tory has made it his life's mission to end illegal discrimination in the banking industry. This book is another step toward that goal.

OPPORTUNITY

So, why did we choose the title *Opportunity*?

As boring and tedious as regulations may seem, sometimes they really do keep things simple and give us insight into the intent. One of the main laws tied to fair lending is the Equal Credit Opportunity Act. Within that name is a key word hidden in plain sight. While we want things to be "equal", that is a result. And obviously, "credit" makes sense because we are talking about lending, but to us, the real driver is the word *opportunity*. What does that mean to provide equal opportunity for credit?

In 2025, Tory had the privilege of giving a TEDx talk on fair lending, inequality, and the racial wealth and home-ownership gaps. If you have not seen it, you can find it on YouTube. In that talk, one of the closing points was simple: not everyone should be approved for a loan. In other words, applicants still need to be creditworthy. They need sufficient income, a history of repayment, and the ability to handle debt responsibly.

But here is the key: everyone who *is* creditworthy should have the same opportunity to apply and be approved. That equal opportunity is not always present, and that is what we hope to help change.

LAYING THE GROUNDWORK

We will return to the *opportunity* theme throughout this book as we explore each stage of the loan life cycle. By the end, you will see how this key word should guide both general lending practices and the design of fair banking programs.

Before we dive deeper, a quick note on terminology. There are many types of organizations that make loans: banks, credit unions, mortgage companies, non-bank institutions, FinTechs, and more. For simplicity, we will use the term "institution" or "organization" to describe any company making loans and when we refer to the person who actually makes the loan, we will call them a "loan officer" or a "lender".

CHAPTER TWO

Compliance Management System

If you have worked for a financial institution in your career, you are likely to have an idea of what a Compliance Management System (CMS) is. If you are directly involved in compliance or audit, you probably have a very good idea about a CMS. Regardless of your background, we want you to think of a CMS as the building blocks of your fair lending program.

We have seen far too many people disregard the importance of building a strong CMS. They feel it is a task of going through the motions to keep regulators happy. Policies are often copied and pasted or purchased from a vendor and rubber-stamped annually. Nobody takes the time to write out good procedures, or more notably, they do not even understand everything that is considered procedures. Training becomes checking boxes, monitoring becomes filling out checklists, and a good quality fair lending audit is a myth. Your CMS elements serve as controls over your fair lending risk, and the larger and more complex your institution, the more important effective controls become.

While the concepts of a CMS are simple, it is a large and complex idea. If you work in a multi-billion-dollar organization, your CMS needs to cover many areas, products, employees, and markets. The CMS governing your fair lending program is one small part of it. However, we are going to focus on the concepts of a fair lending CMS, since this is a fair lending book. You can still take these concepts and apply them to any part of your bank.

What is in a CMS, and why does it matter?

BOARD AND MANAGEMENT OVERSIGHT

The first part is your Board and senior management oversight. If your organization does not have a Board of Directors, that is fine. Think of this group as your executive management and key decision-makers overseeing your organization. If they have the authority to write policy on how you operate in the financial and lending space, they are likely a member of this group. For the purposes of this discussion, we will just call them management.

What is expected of management, and what is their role? They are table setters. They may not be the "boots on the ground" while managing the day-to-day fair lending function of your institution, but they ensure all of the pieces are in place for your organization to be successful. One of their biggest jobs is allocating resources to your compliance program. That can mean hiring compliance professionals and giving them the resources needed to do the job, making sure you have enough people to manage your program, ensuring you have the software you need, or engaging an outside audit firm to help you identify risks and fix issues.

When it comes to having the right-sized team, we have seen over and over again that organizations experiencing quick, significant growth often fail to build up their support teams. We had one client that grew from $300 million in assets to over $1 billion in a matter of a few years. Most of this growth was organic, not through mergers and acquisitions (M&As). This was great for the institution: surging revenue, loan growth, new locations, and all of the other benefits that come with growth.

The problem? They forgot that all of that newfound revenue and profit come with additional expenses in non-revenue generating areas. It is usually compliance, audit, accounting, human resources, and operations personnel that see their team size stay stagnant while loan officers, marketing, and other revenue generators are going gangbusters hiring new staff. If you are a person working for an organization that has experienced this, and you are reading this right now, we have to imagine you are pulling out the highlighter. It is okay; you are not the only one.

This client of ours had one person running the whole compliance department, doing all audits, all file reviews, and they served as the bank's Community Reinvestment Act Officer and Bank Secrecy Act Officer. For those unfamiliar with all of these jobs, most institutions that size have four to six people doing all of them! Guess what happened as a result?

They hired our consulting company to help with compliance reviews, and in the few short months from when they signed an engagement with us to our first review, the compliance officer quit. We were not surprised as this person was completely overworked. Fortunately, they found a new rock star to take over. Then this person also lasted a single year before quitting.

All along, we are telling them they need more people, but they still put it all on one person. Finally, when we were on the third compliance officer in barely 14 months, they listened. The takeaway? Act Your Asset Size! This institution was not a $300 million institution anymore. When you experience significant growth, make sure your support staff is not drowning. The proactive way to find that out is to ask them and ask your peers what they have for support staff. A reactive way to find out is to decide how many people you are willing to let quit before you expand.

We are not picking on executives here. They have a duty to set policy and provide a return to investors, but all of those increased profits and returns also come with additional cost. That is the tradeoff. Eventually, these institutions figured it out, but why not be proactive and grow your support teams with the rest of the organization? We have seen too many great professionals leave because their institution took too long to realize the support teams were drowning.

In addition to ensuring you have enough staff, management also allocates resources for outside assistance. This often comes in the form of an audit or consulting company with expertise in certain areas. That is what we have done for many years as consultants, and it can be a great and cost-effective way to bring in expertise you do not currently have. It can also supplement your internal program and monitoring efforts.

Management should also direct policy at your organization. While certain members of management may not be sitting down and writing details into a fair lending policy, they should have input and be reviewing those policies at least annually.

Management also sets the culture at your organization. We have already talked about proactive and reactive management, but what does that really mean when it comes to fair lending? A proactive institution does not wait around for regulators to force them to do things; they just do it. They hire the right people, train them, and give them the resources to do their jobs. They are the first to learn about regulatory changes, they do not need to be told to buy software, and they know when it is time to get outside help. A proactive institution is always ahead of the game and well prepared for anything that comes up.

A reactive management team, on the other hand, is finding out about issues for the first time in a regulatory examination. We have seen regulatory changes that were two or three years old that management had no idea about. During exams, we have seen some of the weakest fair lending programs while watching the management team sit on their hands with absolutely no idea the house is on fire. This type of culture often needs to be forced to change.

Prior to being consultants, we were both federal regulators. We were commissioned as examiners with the FDIC, and that is where we really learned the trade. We are both so grateful for our time there, and the experience is invaluable. As an examiner, you are in training for several years. Once you meet all your requirements, complete all required classes, and pass the final exam, you become commissioned as a federal bank examiner. At that point, you serve as the examiner-in-charge, or EIC. You are now the one running the exam team, and it is all on your shoulders.

One of Tory's favorite examples of a reactive management team was only his second examination as the EIC. He literally was not commissioned long enough to bake a loaf of bread, and he gets put in charge of this extremely challenging bank examination nobody saw coming. Tory asked for all the pre-examination documents, which many of you who have been examined are used to. With that, he asked for the board minutes and was told, "You can review them onsite." He tried getting clarification and was met with, "You will see when you get here." "Alright, I'm nothing if not adaptable" thought Tory.

After getting to the bank and getting settled in, the compliance officer hands Tory this old, smelly, green-covered book full of pages that literally snaps open like a three-ring binder. What was in this old book you might be asking yourself? It held their board minutes. The person responsible for taking minutes at board meetings refused to use a computer, so he opened this book, fed a sheet of paper into his typewriter, and typed out the minutes. This was 2012. Microsoft Word, already a two-decade-old product, was apparently too cutting-edge a technology. Needless to say, we had major violations in every area we touched.

The kicker was this bank paid for an excellent audit that discovered all these problems. We did not even have to test everything. We already knew where the issues were. However, they had fixed nothing. A six-month-old audit report sat without a single issue being fixed. The only positive thing we gave them credit for was the audit. That was satisfactory, but management was reactive because they failed to fix any of the issues identified.

COMPLIANCE PROGRAM

The second piece of your CMS is your program, and it is broken down into four parts:
- Policies and Procedures
- Training
- Monitoring and Audit
- Consumer Complaints

Fair Lending Related Policies and Procedures
Your fair lending-related policies are where your program starts. This helps establish the culture at your organization.

What are examples of fair lending-related policies? Some are obvious, and some not so much. Yes, if you have a policy called "Fair Lending Policy," you are probably on the right track. We have seen all kinds of variations, and generally fair lending policies are those that cover both lending and fair treatment of customers. We would lump your loan policy into fair lending because it tells your loan officers how to make loans at your organization. Sometimes we do not see a standalone fair lending policy but a fair lending section in a loan policy; that is just fine, especially for smaller institutions with only a few branches. As you become larger and more complex, it might be time to split it out.

Fair lending policies can also include things like a social media policy. Had you asked us just five years ago if a social media policy was critical to a lending institution, we would have brushed it off with a casual "no." Now, it may be one of the most important fair lending-related policies at any lending organization. And when we say social media policy, we do not just mean guidance on social media use during work time. We mean what is expected of every employee, even on their personal social media pages.

We have seen a banker, someone who works in administration and not even a loan officer, make a very discriminatory comment on her own social media page about a political candidate. We do not know this person, so we will give her the benefit of the doubt. Perhaps it was her first time on the internet, but this comment blew up! It was so bad that the local news did a story: "Local banker makes discriminatory comment on Facebook." It was talked about for weeks, and the institution even had a message on their home page about how it was being handled.

We also heard about a commercial lender offering his commentary on a Facebook political post. Evidently, someone made their political views known in a public forum. Turns out, some disagreed and offered rebuttals (we know this already sounds made up, but we promise it happened.) Before you know it, there were 300 comments on this post. We would love to tell you these were mature, well-crafted political arguments that changed minds forever. Of course not, this was a bunch of people just yelling at each other. But this commercial lender offered his opinion: "You people need to go back to your country." If you are reading this book, you are likely an adult and know exactly what he meant. Guess what? Everyone else did too. Someone screenshotted it, sent it to the CEO, and said, "You have a racist lender at your organization!" Now what do you do? This is why a social media policy is so important. Set expectations and require all employees to read it and sign it annually.

There is another crazy concept we come across a lot. When our company does fair lending audits, and we do them often, we interview lenders. One of our questions is, "Do you have a social media policy?" Of course, we already know the answer, but we want to see if they actually know about the policy. About 20 percent of the time, they are unaware. About 70 percent of the time, they do know it exists but the last time they read it was during orientation roughly 12 years ago. What good is a policy if nobody has read it in years? It seems only about 10 percent of the time do they know about it and read it annually.

Social media continually evolves. Myspace once dominated the market, and now most people under the age of 20 have never even heard of it. A strong social media policy that encompasses online content and activity is key to helping control the risk.

If fair lending-related policies give guidance on how your organization operates, procedures are often step-by-step guidelines on how you actually do your job. These can be written guidelines, checklists, software, or other informal guidance your staff follow.

Procedures can be written or unwritten. The smallest institutions, often with only a few or one location and a handful of loan officers, can get by without a lot of written procedures. Many of the loan officers have been around for years, and changes to policies and procedures can be quickly decided and communicated to a few individuals. It is easier to have control over a loan program with only a few individuals making loan decisions. While many of the procedures on how lenders do their jobs may not be formally written down, they are still procedures and reflect your CMS.

As institutions grow larger and more complex, there is a greater need to formalize procedures. How your organization sets interest rates on loans is a perfect example of a critical fair lending procedure. This can be as simple as an interest rate sheet that changes periodically with changes in market rates. That is a basic fair lending procedure.

For a small institution with five loan officers, it is not as critical to have a formalized rate sheet. We have seen many of these small institutions have a "base rate" they price from on loans. Imagine now an organization with 10 or 100 branches and 100 or 1,000 loan officers. In these cases, you need very specific procedures on how lenders do their jobs or they will be pricing all over the place without any consistency.

Other fair lending procedures include how a lender underwrites loans. These procedures can be a checklist, an Excel workbook, or a software program where a lender or underwriter enters the customer's data to calculate ratios and make conclusions on credit decisions. There are many different types of underwriting models, but one thing remains the same: clear and concise policies and procedures are the best way to build and maintain a strong lending and fair lending program.

Think of it this way: there are legal and illegal ways to discriminate against someone. Illegal ways include the prohibited basis characteristics under the fair lending laws: race, ethnicity, age, sex, and others. A lender can never factor those into a credit decision. In fact, when building or auditing a fair lending program, the whole goal is to review and ensure you are not making credit decisions based on these illegal factors.

What are the legal ways to discriminate? Those are your underwriting factors. Lenders should use data and metrics like credit score, income, repayment ability, or collateral value to make loan decisions. If you think of those as your legal forms of discrimination, you will see how critical it is to clearly define them. Clearly defined policies and procedures are the best way to build a strong fair lending program.

We have seen many examples of unclear policies and procedures, and anyone performing a fair lending program review or audit should be looking for just that. What are some examples? We are glad you asked.

"No recent late payments." We saw this in an underwriting checklist once. Cool. As a loan officer, I will be sure to follow my institution's policy and check for recent late payments. Wait, what is recent? The policy does not define it, so every loan officer will make up their own definition. Some may think 3 months is recent while others may think 24 months is acceptable. Do you see how unclear that is?

We now have loan officers making all kinds of different decisions, and there is a major risk that their decisions may impact one prohibited basis negatively. The reason is that lenders may subconsciously look at white borrowers and think 3 or 6 months of no late payments is reasonable but then a minority borrower is held to a higher standard of 24 months. While it is not often intentional, it is still illegal discrimination. Therein lies the problem. Had that policy or procedure been written crystal clear, we would eliminate the chance for illegal discrimination.

We have also seen procedures that talk about how to underwrite a luxury car. The first question we asked is what is a luxury car? That should be defined, but it was not. We have also seen "Classic Car" in pricing standards. What is considered a classic car? In South Dakota, where Tory lives, a classic car is defined as one 25 years old or older. That is specific; the label "Classic Car" is not.

Clearly defined policies and procedures are key and an early step, but actually following the guidance is just as critical. You can have the most beautifully written fair lending policy and procedural guidance, if you think such things are beautiful, and as fair lending professionals, we do. But if they are never followed, they lose nearly all their value. We will talk a lot more about not following policies and procedures when we discuss policy exceptions.

Fair Lending Related Training
Of your CMS program components related to fair lending, fair lending training is likely the most obvious to figure out. Training includes any fair lending-related training such as online course modules and webinars. Those are likely the most common types of training most employees get. They cover the basics, such as laws and regulations, definitions of discrimination, and sometimes a few case studies. This training is okay. It checks boxes, but does it really teach your loan staff how fair lending should work?

Expand what you think fair lending training is or can be. Let's start with basic lender training. Think of this as teaching lenders the basics of how they do their jobs. How are they supposed to underwrite and price loans? What is the process for having borderline credit decisions or denials approved? How do they get a policy exception approved?

What is acceptable and unacceptable social media behavior?

Thinking of basic lender training as fair lending training makes sense if you see that your policies and procedures are the building blocks of your fair lending program and your management-approved legal forms of discrimination. If strong policies and procedures are how you ensure lenders do not discriminate, it is not a stretch to think that you should do extensive and frequent training in these critical areas.

We have developed a concept we call the "Swap-a-Lender" example. Let's say you ask a loan officer from a competitor down the street to come into your organization and work for a day. This loan officer has 15 years of lending experience, so they are not new to making loans and know the basics of credit. They do not need to be taught those things. However, they have no idea how to make a loan at your organization.

You sit them in an office for the day and only give them your written policies and procedures on how to make loans. They are not allowed to ask any questions, only gaining knowledge from what they read in your written program. Then, you send 20 loan applicants to them that day. Would they be able to make the same fair and consistent decisions all day long only based on what they learned from reading policies and procedures? Would they know the proper way to calculate a debt-to-income ratio or what valuation model to use to price a used car loan? Would they know how to price loans or how to ask for a rate exception?

That is the Swap-a-Lender concept in a nutshell, and it helps illustrate both the need for clearly written guidance and training on that guidance for your loan staff. Spend the time teaching your lenders the basics of how to do their jobs. Do not assume they know just because they have a lot of experience in credit.

Fair Lending Related Monitoring/Audit

Monitoring and audit accomplish the same goal: using reviews and testing to ensure you have a strong fair lending program. However, there are two quite different ways to get there. They each have their pros and cons.

An analogy to explain the difference is to think of monitoring as brushing your teeth each day. It helps keep your teeth clean and greatly reduces the chances of cavities or oral disease.

An audit is like going to the dentist every six months. The dentist does a thorough review of your oral health, helps identify ways you can do things better, fixes any major issues, and is really your expert to ensure healthy teeth and gums.

While many people fear the dentist, it is easy to agree that good oral health makes trips to the dentist much less stressful. In other words, the better monitoring program you have, the better your audits will turn out.

What does fair lending monitoring look like? Think of it as your daily or weekly checks on your program to ensure things are operating as designed. Sometimes monitoring efforts are formal, documented, and utilized checklists. Reviewing adverse action notices before they go out to a denied applicant is a great example of fair lending monitoring.

You get 30 days to communicate a credit decision, and most of the time, denied loan applications are a clear-cut denial decision. There is not a lot of guesswork; however, completing the denial process, thoroughly documenting the denial decision, and completing and mailing out the adverse action notice are several tedious steps you want to get right. If you have a trained compliance professional or other loan personnel with a good quality checklist review all files before the adverse action notice is sent to the denied loan applicant, you have a chance to catch and fix technical issues or violations.

That is an example of the effectiveness of monitoring: it is timely, gives immediate feedback on your program, and can help prevent violations from happening.

Audits are much more in-depth and really dig into a program and data, but they are often not timely. Audits are a point-in-time pause to review the last 3, 6, or perhaps 12 months (or longer) of your performance.

During a fair lending audit, we often transaction test a sample of adverse action notices. If we review 10 of them and find no technical issues, that tells us that either you have good procedures to ensure they are filled out right, people are well-trained in the process, or your monitoring is catching issues and fixing them before they go out the door. Or it also could be a combination of all three.

However, if we find many technical issues, that means there is a breakdown somewhere earlier in the process. Those technical issues are now regulatory violations, and there is no way to fix them. Yes, you can identify the root cause and prevent future occurrences, but there is no way to go back and fix a preventable issue because required compliance deadlines have already passed.

As we have already stated, the better monitoring you have in place, the smoother your audits will go and, ultimately, the better your examinations will turn out.

The adverse action example is a great way to illustrate the difference between monitoring and audit, but what are other examples of fair lending monitoring? A secondary review of loan files is a common one. Simply reviewing loan files to ensure that all procedures were followed is a great way to ensure your procedures are clearly written, consistently followed, and your loan officers are trained.

This could be as simple as ensuring the correct interest rate was quoted and all underwriting criteria were accurately followed. If you pull three credit scores and your procedures say to use the middle one, ensure that is what happened. Maybe verify that a debt-to-income ratio was correctly calculated. If someone asked for a policy exception, ensure they followed protocol and received the proper approval. Those are simple daily checks on loan files that can be done to ensure fair and consistent loan decisions are made.

Clear and concise policies and procedures are the best way to build a strong fair lending program but consistently following them is just as critical. Simple monitoring to ensure they are being followed is one of the easiest ways to strengthen your CMS and help prevent fair lending issues.

While determining what truly is fair lending monitoring can be open to a bit of interpretation, fair lending audits are a bit more straightforward.

First of all, how often should you do a fair lending audit? Well, that depends on several factors: How big is your organization? Where do you operate? What types of loan products do you offer? How many lenders do you have? Who makes credit decisions? And maybe the biggest one of all - how strong is your fair lending program? There are really only a few ways to determine the strength of your program. A thorough fair lending audit or a regulatory exam are the most common.

Allow us to digress for a moment and talk about regulatory fair lending exams but keep this in mind for any type of exam. If we had a nickel for every time someone said to us, "The examiners never said anything, so it must be good," we would have a heavy bag full of nickels, though not a lot of money.

Stop thinking that just because something was not identified, or the examiners did not say anything, that there cannot be a problem. Why? First of all, examiners do not look at everything! They cannot possibly do a full, extensive audit of your program. There simply is not enough time. In fact, they are not auditing at all. That is why they do not call it an audit; they call it an examination. They transaction test high-risk areas to determine the strength or weakness of your program, but they cannot test everything.

Here is another hot take: examiners miss things, and they do not know everything. Maybe you had an examiner reviewing an area for their second time in their career. Maybe they did not know a certain part of the regulatory requirement. Maybe they did not review an area at all that you thought they did.

Examiners are extremely well-trained and we know that for a fact because we both spent years training to become one. We spent months of our lives in schools and training sessions and years in banks receiving hands-on training to get our commission. But we are still human.

The exam process is limited by resource allocation, so there is only so much they can do with the time that they have. That is why a strong CMS makes examinations go so smoothly, and monitoring and audit are key to that. If one of us is the EIC of your exam, and we see you have excellent policies and procedures, well-trained staff, consistent and thorough monitoring, and a strong audit program, we just need to do enough testing to verify that. That is why brushing and flossing daily makes the trip to the dentist so much easier. Stop thinking of an examination as an audit. It is not, and it is often not even close to the same thing.

Back to the audit timing discussion. How often should

you get a fair lending audit? The smallest and least complex banks sometimes never do a fair lending audit. Those are rural institutions with simple products, few branches and loan officers, good procedures, and low risk for illegal discrimination. We are not saying they should never do fair lending audits, but we have seen many small institutions not necessarily needing one.

Most medium-sized institutions typically do an annual audit, and they often outsource the audit. They do not have staff well-versed in fair lending audits, and they may not have fair lending software to review their performance. Once a year, a company like ours will come in and do a thorough audit. We look at all of the loan lifecycle risks we will be covering in this book, read policies and procedures, interview staff, and review lending performance through HMDA and other data.

The largest institutions do a combination of robust internal audits and external engagements. They may be doing quarterly audits in some areas and as often as monthly in others. They often audit lending departments separately and will do a thorough review of each major market. Fair lending software is no longer optional for these organizations, and well-trained audit staff and good external partnerships are key to reviewing such a large and complex program.

The last thing to note about both monitoring and audit is they can never be the root cause of issues at your organization. That means when either process identifies issues, some breakdown prior to that led to the issue. Either there was no proper asset allocation to prevent it, clear policies and procedures to guide staff, or effective training to ensure the issue did not happen. Something prior to finding it in monitoring or audit is always the root cause.

If you are reading this and work in monitoring or audit, you might find a little comfort in that way of thinking, but it also puts extra pressure on you because you are the last line of defense to identify issues. If a problem happens in your fair lending program and monitoring or audit did not identify it, you can still be blamed for being ineffective, even though you were not the source of the issue.

Response to Fair Lending Related Consumer Complaints

The last part of your CMS program has to do with complaints. For the smallest lending organizations, you may go years without a complaint. For the largest, you may get several each day.

In general, all lending organizations that have sufficient complaint volume should be monitoring that data and reviewing trends. Speaking broadly about banking, and not specifically fair lending, you should monitor complaints to find weaknesses in your overall program that covers all products and services. That does not mean any single complaint is not critical, but 10 to 20 complaints about a fee on a checking account may indicate that your disclosures are not clear or your marketing did not properly communicate that fee.

When it comes to fair lending-related complaints, they tend to be specific to one person and one event. Someone had a bad experience with your loan staff, and they have reason to believe they were discriminated against illegally. You do not often see multiple fair lending complaints that are closely related unless it is related to a common message like a marketing advertisement. However, it is possible to see a fair lending complaint for a lending organization that is failing or refusing to lend fairly and consistently across its geographic footprint. These types of complaints often come from community groups or organizations that have reviewed and are criticizing your performance using publicly available HMDA data.

Regardless of the complaint, fair lending related complaints should be taken very seriously. They should receive prompt attention, thorough research, and an appropriate response. We have seen one fair lending complaint drive an entire fair lending examination. That is how critical they are.

While complaints are unflattering, they are a critical component of your CMS because they are outside feedback on how you are performing.

Risk Assessments

Performing a fair lending risk assessment is a great way to help you pull this all together. A risk assessment should look at potential fair lending risk, review your controls, and give you a good picture of where you should focus resources.

The first thing you need to do is understand your up-front, or inherent risk. This is the risk present in your program before you do anything. It can include things like the products you offer. If you offer non-traditional or riskier products, your inherent risk can increase. It also includes the areas you serve. If you operate in major metropolitan areas with diverse populations, things like redlining risk go way up.

Your controls are the next part. This is where your CMS elements come into play. If you have strong written guidance, well trained people, continually monitor loan decisions and data, and perform quality periodic audits, you can help reduce much of your fair lending risk. If, however, you do not have a strong CMS in place, those high inherent risk areas remain high, and your CMS, or controls, do little to reduce it.

Lastly, we have your residual risk. This is the inherent risk level, reduced by the effectiveness of your controls, and leaves you with the risk left over, or what is residual. The goal is to always have low residual risk, but sometimes that may not be achievable. In those cases, you want to ensure you are dedicating the appropriate resources to manage the residual fair lending risk.

For the smallest and least complex institutions, a fair lending risk assessment may be a small part of an overall risk assessment or may not even exist. For large and complex institutions, a fair lending risk assessment is one of the key tools in your risk toolbox. Not sure if you need a risk assessment? Everyone should do something. Even small organizations can develop a basic fair lending risk assessment. The complexity of it and the effort you put in should match the size and complexity of your institution. Do not worry; if you are not sure you need a risk assessment, the regulators will surely let you know.

CMS – A LINE OF COMPLIANCE

We view a CMS as a linear process.

First – Your Board and senior management set the table for compliance. They approve policies and procedures, allocate resources, and help establish a culture of compliance.

Second – Your policies and procedures tell employees how to do their jobs. This is your first line of defense against regulatory issues, technical violations, and fair lending discrimination. Properly crafted and consistently followed, they can prevent a host of issues.

Third – Training your staff is crucial for fair lending success. Even with excellent policies and procedures and a pro-active, supportive culture, if your employees do not know how to properly do their jobs, the previous components will be ineffective.

Fourth – Monitoring is critical to determining the continual health of your fair lending program. It is the easiest way to get timely feedback and make changes when things are not working.

Fifth – Periodic audits are a good time to pause and see how the program is working. When you look at data daily in monitoring, you cannot see trends develop. When you look at the past year, you get a much better picture of where your organization is heading.

Sixth – Consumer complaints are somewhat outside this linear cycle from the standpoint that you should never rely on complaints to be the primary source to identify issues. However, they act as an additional line of defense to identify issues in your program, as long as you are listening and paying attention to the complaint or complaint trends.

CMS WRAP UP

Your CMS is a living, breathing thing that should constantly be improved. Dedicating both resources and intent to your program is critical to its continued success. That means when you grow, make sure your CMS grows with you. Look for ways to make your policies and procedures better. Invest in your people to ensure they are highly skilled and trained. Highly skilled individuals also do a much better job monitoring and auditing your program. A robust complaint process helps round it all out.

There are other components to your CMS that you should also consider. A big one is regulatory change management. Ensure you keep up with changes to regulations and guidance and know that interpretations can change over time. This ties back to a proactive versus reactive compliance posture. If you are always learning about regulatory changes in an exam, you are likely reactive. If you are prepared and have a program in place to adapt, you are likely proactive.

Third-party risk is also a major component for some organizations. You can hire third parties to help you both manage your program and offer products and services to your customers. FinTech partnerships have become increasingly common as they allow an organization to partner and offer lending products and services, they would never be able to do on their own. It is critical to remember that you are responsible for everything those third parties do on your behalf. Their CMS becomes your CMS, and if they do not have robust policies and procedures, well-trained staff, and a strong monitoring and audit program in place, their fair lending problems will become your fair lending problems.

We are going to talk about many fair lending concepts in this book, but every single one, every single risk, and every single problem can potentially be tied back to your CMS. Always look to identify problems and look to see if a CMS breakdown led to the problem. That is how you build a strong fair lending program to prevent future issues.

Tory has a life mantra for himself and the people he leads – it is okay to make mistakes. We are human, so they will happen, but please try not to repeat them.

If you do not fix your CMS when problems arise, you will be doomed to repeat them.

CHAPTER THREE

Application Risk

LOAN LIFECYCLE

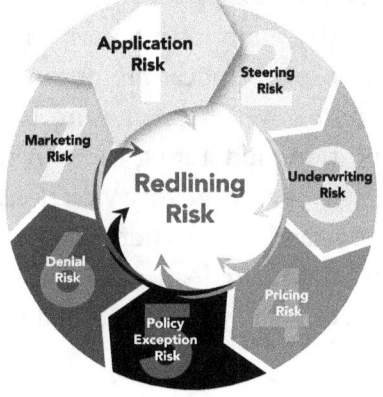

Welcome to the start of the loan lifecycle of fair lending risks - the application process.

Yes, it could be said that marketing often kicks off the loan lifecycle, and that is often true. But we will leave marketing for the end so that we can first learn about the different fair lending risks and then use marketing as a tool to help mitigate them.

There are many fair lending risks present during the application process. The first is the application form used. If a lender is taking an application for a home secured loan, they must collect government monitoring information from the applicant. In other words, they must request the applicant's race, ethnicity, and sex. If a lender does not use the right application, those questions likely will not be asked, and that creates regulatory violations.

On the flip side, the opposite problem can occur. If a lender uses a home loan application for someone wanting to buy a vehicle, those government monitoring questions will be on the application, and asking them in that situation is illegal. So now they have regulatory violations the other way, by requesting information the lender is not supposed to collect. The lesson: make sure loan officers use the right form for the right type of loan every time to reduce risk.

SCREENING APPLICANTS

One of the biggest risks we have seen in the application process is older than the loan application forms themselves, but it still happens every single day, and that is screening.

What do we mean by screening? A lender screens an applicant when they ask upfront questions to understand the applicant's creditworthiness. This is not inherently wrong. In fact, it is part of most application processes. However, it becomes an issue when the loan officer then discourages an applicant from continuing the application process if they do not like what they hear.

Here's an example. Tory came into your office wanting to buy a new car. He sat down with a lender and casually mentioned that he checked his credit score the week prior, and it was not good; it was 490. See, Tory does not like to pay his bills on time, and evidently that is not good for his credit score.

Let's say the minimum credit score your organization will approve for a new car purchase is 620. The loan officer knows that Tory is so far below your credit score standards that there is no way they will lend him a nickel, let alone $50,000 for a new car. They say, "You will not qualify for a car loan, so there is no point in applying."

What's the problem here?

The problem is that Tory came in to apply for a loan, he communicated creditworthiness information to your lender, and they communicated back a credit decision. Do you think he is going to sit down and fill out an application after that? Of course not. That also means he will never get an adverse action notice (denial letter), so it is like the application process never happened, but in fact, it 100 percent did happen.

Let's take the example a step further. Suppose Tory wanted to refinance his home and casually mentioned that he filed for bankruptcy last year. The home loan officer knows there is no way he will qualify for a refinance, so they discourage him from applying. Not only does he not fill out an application and not get an adverse action notice, but that ap-

plication will also never end up on the institution's HMDA
Loan Application Register (LAR). Now we have even bigger
regulatory issues that extend past fair lending.

Organizations that screen applicants and discourage
those most likely to be denied are creating several problems.
First, their HMDA data is inaccurate. They are under-
reporting denials, which artificially inflate their origination
rates while deflating their denial rates. This affects their fair
lending performance, and if you are a peer institution in
their market, it affects yours as well. You are compared to
how peers in your area perform, and if their data is inaccurate and artificially inflated, your numbers look worse by
comparison.

Second, the institution now has a HMDA omissions
problem. Examiners perform two separate HMDA data
validation tests prior to an examination. If you have ever
wondered why examiners often come a few months early to
review HMDA data, it is to make sure that data is accurate
enough to use for the exam.

The first test is the one you are probably familiar with –
data accuracy. This is where they review the LAR and loan
files to ensure the data in the files matches what was reported. Someone at your organization likely does this throughout the year. We call it scrubbing HMDA data (It is a ton of
fun if you have never been involved).

The second test is an omissions test. Here, examiners look
to see if HMDA-reportable applications have been left off
your LAR, or "omitted." The easiest way to do this is to request
your loan download. This is a history of all originated loans,
usually in Excel spreadsheet format. They comb through it to
find dwelling-secured loans that may not be on your LAR,
and they review your denial files to see if there are adverse

action notices for dwelling-secured loans not included on the LAR. The whole point of an omissions review is to ensure you have reported all HMDA-reportable applications. Let's say they do not find any missing. They conclude that all originated loans and all dwelling-secured adverse action notices are on your LAR. You are in the clear, right? Not so fast. How could an examiner know your HMDA data is still inaccurate or in this case, incomplete? One way is to look at your denial rate and compare it to other similarly situated institutions.

For example, if you made 1,000 loans in a year and have only 4 denials, you are either the most generous institution on the planet, in which case, please call us because we have a $100 million commercial loan application we would love to submit, or your lenders are screening applicants and discouraging people from applying.

If that happens, it can also be uncovered through interviews. We recently performed a fair lending review of a nationwide mortgage institution, and during the review, we conducted nearly a dozen interviews with lenders, underwriters, and members of management. Several lenders cited weaknesses in their HMDA data collection process. Some said it was just easier to fill out the form themselves rather than ask the applicant. Others said they simply check the box that the applicant "did not wish to provide" monitoring information. One lender even walked us through their process and told us flat out that they tell applicants to withdraw their applications if they do not believe the applicant will be approved by the underwriting department.

This situation was a bit unique because the client had instructed all staff to be open and honest with us so they could get to the root cause of their issues. Most lenders will not admit these kinds of facts to examiners, as we would not either, but that is beside the point.

This organization clearly had HMDA data collection problems, and that data flows directly into their fair lending reviews. They recently paid a different firm for an annual fair lending audit that was quite expensive, and they had no idea that their data was inaccurate, making the findings and conclusions from this very expensive audit unreliable. There is no way to get a clear and accurate picture of fair lending performance on HMDA-reportable loans without full and accurate data.

The third point we want to illustrate ties back to the book's title - *Opportunity*.

There is no more critical point during the loan lifecycle to ensure every applicant has the same equal opportunity to get a loan than during the application process. It is at this step that a lender may discourage an applicant from applying, which means they do not have the same opportunity to go through the underwriting process and receive an accurate and fair decision. Applicants also lose the chance to learn *why* they were denied (assuming they actually get denied), which prevents them from improving those areas and increasing their future approval chances. The "Opportunity" all starts with the application, and everyone needs to be allowed to go through the process. It is literally in the name of the law.

ASSESSING APPLICATION DATA

When you review your HMDA data, there is a lot you can analyze from the application standpoint. You can review your application data to ensure you are receiving applications from individuals at rates that align with your demographic footprint. In other words, if 30 percent of the individuals living in your area are Hispanic, what percentage of applications should you expect from Hispanic individuals? Do you think 22 percent or 32 percent would be reasonable? Likely. But if 30 percent of your area is made up of Hispanic individuals, and 3 percent of all applications come from Hispanic individuals, you likely have problems. As we move through this book and discuss more stages of the loan lifecycle, we will talk about potential root causes of this problem.

The application risk is a great place to start. If you are not receiving applications from minority individuals and high-minority areas at rates that align with census data, it really does not matter much how well you perform on other fair lending tests. Low application rates from minority individuals will always result in low origination rates, meaning your organization is not serving your community's needs. You cannot originate loans without applications (Or at least, we have not figured out how to do that yet).

We have had many lending executives ask us if they can "purchase loans to meet their fair lending obligations." We never know quite how to answer because there are no *fair lending obligations*. There are no metrics, thresholds, or tests to ensure you are lending fairly throughout your geographic footprint. Yes, if you are significantly behind peers in lending to minority individuals and high-minority areas, you may be scrutinized, but there is no magic number you need to hit.

We believe people who ask that question are likely confusing fair lending with the Community Reinvestment Act (CRA). CRA evaluations do look at lending metrics throughout your assessment area, so you could argue that you are lending to "meet your CRA obligations." Personally, we are not fans of that phrase. Reinvesting in your community should not be viewed as an obligation but both a requirement and a privilege. Allowing a financial institution to make loans and serve a community comes with the expectation that they will serve all of that community's residents.

Fair lending does not have tests like CRA. While CRA allows you to purchase loans from other organizations and may give you credit for that during your evaluation period, fair lending does not generally consider purchased loans. Fair lending cares about the organization making the credit decision and ensuring that credit decision is fair and free from discrimination. If your organization purchases loans from another institution, you do not make the credit decision on those loans, so there is nothing to evaluate you from a fair lending perspective. CRA, on the other hand, wants to make sure you extend credit to all parts of your area. If you have loans on your books to low-income families or small businesses, you are extending credit to those groups, even if you did not make the original credit decision, which is why CRA may view that purchased loan favorably.

We believe that is where the confusion usually comes from. Fair lending and CRA may appear similar, but they have drastically different requirements, metrics, and evaluations.

Key Takeaways

Here are some takeaways for you to lower risk in the application process:

- Ensure lenders use the right form for the right loan type every time.

- Train your lenders to encourage everyone to fill out an application and go through the loan process.

- Collect the required demographic information from every applicant every time as the regulation requires. This is the only way you will truly know your fair lending risk.

- Review your application rates from minority individuals and high-minority areas and compare those rates with census demographics and peer data.

CHAPTER FOUR

Steering Risk

LOAN LIFECYCLE

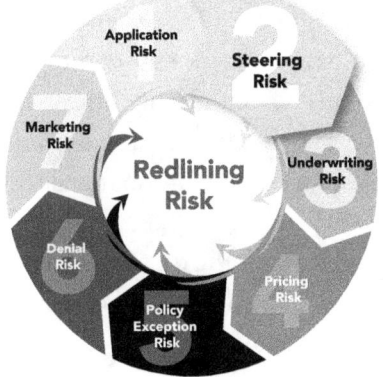

Once you receive an application, the next step is to determine exactly what product your applicant will get. Sometimes this is simple when there is only one viable option, but other times it can be quite complex.

Mortgage lending is one of those complex areas. Will the loan stay in-house or be sold on the secondary market? Does the customer want long-term financing, a shorter-term balloon loan, or perhaps an adjustable-rate loan? Will it be conventional financing or a government-guaranteed loan product?

Even non–real estate secured loans may have different loan choices. Your organization may have different third-party relationships, referral agreements, or sell add-on products with loan options. All of these factors can impact a loan's costs, terms, features, and even who ultimately originates it.

Whenever these types of factors affect what the customer pays for the loan, steering risk enters the picture. Steering is not necessarily bad. When a loan officer helps a customer find the product that best meets their needs, that is a positive, and those are successful financial transactions. But when a loan officer puts a customer into a product that is not the best fit, simply because it increases compensation to the loan officer or the organization, and does so on a prohibited basis, that is potentially illegal.

GOVERNMENT-GUARANTEED LOANS (GGLs)

Let's start with government-guaranteed loans, or GGLs. These include programs like the Federal Housing Administration (FHA), Veterans Affairs (VA), and U.S. Department of Agriculture (USDA) loans. These programs are excellent options for homebuyers who may have lower credit scores or less money saved for a down payment. They can help get applicants into homes when they otherwise would not qualify for conventional financing.

So, what is the problem?

GGL programs often come with an upfront funding fee, and some also include an annual fee. Over the life of the loan, these can add up to a much higher overall cost. When a customer qualifies for both conventional and GGL options but gets steered into the GGL, they may be harmed by being placed into the higher-cost loan option. If this happens on a prohibited basis characteristic, which is fairly common, it becomes a fair lending issue.

The good news is all of this can be reviewed through your HMDA data. The type of loan option a borrower chooses (or in some cases, was chosen for them) is a reportable field under HMDA. Using fair lending software, you can find out whether minority individuals are being steered into GGLs more often than white borrowers. You can also compare your performance to peers, which is one of the best ways to measure this key fair lending risk.

Measuring GGL origination rates by race or ethnicity and comparing them to white borrowers is not always the best indicator of risk. The unfortunate reason for that is the history of discriminatory lending policies that have negatively affected people of color.

In Tory's TEDx talk, he shared statistics and discussed at length how racial discrimination in lending has shaped today's realities and how the racial homeownership and wealth gaps are actually wider today than when redlining was still legal in the 1960s.

If minority individuals were historically denied home-ownership and income disparities restricted home-buying options, those individuals will appear less creditworthy in underwriting analyses. While the color of your skin has no bearing on whether you will pay your bills on time, those key underwriting factors lenders use (that we will discuss in the next chapter) to make credit decisions determine whether someone ever gets a loan. If people of color cannot buy homes, they are forced to rent. Rent payments often do nothing to build credit scores, forcing many borrowers of color to turn to GGLs as their only home-buying option.

That means comparing the rate of white and minority borrowers placed into FHA loans may not always be the best way to determine steering risk. The characteristics of your market may have a higher need for FHA lending, and this is where peer comparisons become most valuable. If your organization's rate of placing minority borrowers into FHA loans is much higher than your peers, you may have heightened steering risk.

In these cases, it is time to present your data to management and have in-depth discussions with loan staff. Maybe there is a valid explanation. For example, perhaps your organization is heavily invested in FHA lending, so your FHA origination rates will naturally be higher than peers. On the other hand, perhaps your loan officers automatically steer minority borrowers into FHA loans without truly considering conventional options. These are the kinds of questions you want to answer yourself and be ready to defend during a fair lending examination.

Perhaps your institution does not offer any GGLs. Is that a problem? It might reduce steering risk, but it can create other issues.

In the previous chapter, we talked about how few denials can signal that applicants are being screened and discouraged from applying. Conversely, high denial rates can also be a warning sign, though not always for the reasons you might think. We once performed a fair lending audit for a billion-dollar regional bank whose denial rate for Black borrowers was three to four times higher than both white borrowers and peers. On the surface, this looked like an underwriting problem. Why were Black borrowers being denied so much more often at this bank than Black borrowers at all other banks in the area? This had to be discrimination, right?

Most people's first instinct is to go straight to a file analysis. Start pulling approved and denied files and comparing credit decisions. But before diving into that fun process, we looked at their GGL data. Since their denial rate for Black borrowers was so high, we wanted to see if those applicants were getting FHA loans at rates consistent with peers. Take a guess at how many FHA or USDA loans they originated. We will give you a hint: it rhymes with zero. That is right; not a single GGL loan to anyone.

While the initial data showed high denial rates, and the automatic assumption is an underwriting problem with a likely file analysis in the near future, the real problem was a lack of product options. Because Black applicants did not generally qualify for conventional loans and there were no GGL options available, they were simply turned down. Had this bank offered GGL options, they likely would have originated many more loans, their denial rates would have been in line with peers, and they would have better served the customers in their community.

Back to the Community Reinvestment Act (CRA) for a

moment. The CRA is not just cleverly named; what you are supposed to do is literally in the name. You are supposed to reinvest in your community.

Since this bank did not offer products to meet the needs of its community, it could easily face criticism in a CRA evaluation. This example shows exactly why it is so important to understand the entire loan lifecycle of risks, not just jump straight into a file review. This bank had a strong underwriting program and followed it consistently, but it failed to offer products and services that truly served its community.

There are situations where a customer qualifies for both a GGL and conventional financing and chooses the GGL route. Tory is a perfect example of that situation.

In his late 20's, Tory was an Air Force veteran buying his first home. He was not thrilled about draining his savings for a big down payment or paying private mortgage insurance (PMI), so he looked at the VA loan option. It required a few thousand dollars upfront for the funding fee, but it offered 100 percent financing with no PMI. Plus, he could do interest rate reduction loans in the future as rates were dropping with no additional cost. For Tory, the VA loan was the best option.

What should a loan officer do in that situation? It is simple: document it. The borrower qualified for both a conventional loan and a VA loan. He chose the VA loan because of these reasons. It really is that simple. Documentation like that is critical, because if your GGL rates are high and examiners perform a file analysis, those comments help tell your story.

One of the best ways we have seen institutions reduce steering risk around GGLs is to provide anti-steering documentation. This usually includes a product matrix that spells out the different product options, the costs, and the benefits. They also train loan officers to have in-depth conversations with loan applicants to determine each of the product options they qualify for and educate borrowers so they can make the best decision that meets their needs.

PRODUCT CHANNELS AND COMPENSATION

Your product option channels can also create steering risk. Some institutions have different departments or divisions where loan officers can direct customers. When those product options vary in terms and cost, steering risk can increase. The same goes for third-party product channels. If you can refer customers to different external options, and loan officers receive compensation for those referrals, your steering risk rises.

Steering risk really comes down to what the borrower pays, the terms they get, and maybe most importantly, what the loan officer gets paid. If a loan officer can make more money by steering applicants into certain products, there is a strong incentive to do so. That is where you often see disproportionate numbers of prohibited basis group individuals being funneled into higher-cost products. This is also where steering risk overlaps with redlining risk.

If your product analysis by race, ethnicity, or gender shows that minority or female borrowers disproportionately receive higher-cost products, you have heightened steering risk. If, geographically, you see high-cost products concentrated in high-minority areas while low-cost products are concentrated in low-minority areas, now you are seeing steering risk leading to redlining risk.

While mortgage loan originator compensation rules

restrict such practices, other products, especially consumer and commercial loans, may still allow for compensation structures that pose this risk. As a compliance professional or auditor, you must understand your organization's lending compensation practices to ensure lenders are not incentivized to steer customers toward specific products for personal gain. If they are, monitoring those practices is critical to controlling risk.

ADD-ON PRODUCTS

The last area of steering risk to understand involves add-on products, or ancillary products sold with a loan. The most common are credit life and credit disability insurance. These policies ensure that debt is covered if the borrower dies or becomes disabled. They can provide security for families, but they also come at a cost.

In our experience, institutions usually take one of two approaches: they either go all in or nothing at all. If an institution decides to offer these products, they often push staff to solicit them every time. We have seen institutions where lenders sell one of these products on more than 50 percent of loans. On the other hand, many institutions do not offer them at all, while some others offer them only as an accommodation.

If you are an institution that does not offer add-on products, this is a risk that you do not need to worry about. If you offer them but rarely sell any, your risk is also low.

We worked with a billion-dollar bank that always offered add-on products. Each year during our fair lending audit, we asked how many policies they sold. The answer was usually around five. Finally, we asked why they even offered the products if they never sold them. They got the message, and that was the last year they offered credit life or credit disability policies.

Credit life and disability insurance are not the only add-on products. Some institutions sell GAP insurance for vehicle loans, which protects borrowers if their car is totaled or stolen and they owe more than it is worth. If the car is worth $20,000 but the borrower owes $25,000, the GAP insurance covers the "gap", so they do not pay out of pocket to cover the loan for a car that no longer has value or utility.

Other add-on products include credit monitoring or identity theft protection. These can help protect consumers whose identities are stolen, something that can take months or years to fix and cost a great deal of time and money. Some institutions sell this alongside loans, while others sell it independently.

Whether or not your organization sells add-on products is a management decision. Opinions on these products vary widely as some view them as predatory, a way to make extra money, while others swear by their value and share personal stories about how they have protected families financially. Whatever side of that debate you fall on, if you sell add-on products, there are specific steps you should take to reduce your fair lending risk.

Just like with GGLs, the risk here is disproportionately steering minority or female borrowers into these products. For example, only selling credit life insurance to women but not men, or only soliciting add-ons in high-minority areas. Knowing how your loan officers are compensated is also key, even if the commissions are small. Over time, those small amounts can add up for high-volume loan officers.

Here is how to set up a strong CMS:

1. Have clear procedures for add-on sales. The best approach is consistency. Lenders should either offer it every time or not offer it at all. Those who never offer it at all will have very few sales, usually from borrowers who request it, and risk is low. Even where sales are high, if products are offered the same way every time to all borrowers, risk is also lower.

2. Train your loan staff. Strong policies and procedures are only effective if staff know and understand them. Train your lenders on product offerings and sales procedures, and the same applies to GGLs. Lay out all product options for applicants so they can make informed decisions that best meet their needs.

3. Monitor. Track add-on product sales history and perform basic analyses on who is buying these products and under what circumstances.

Key Takeaways

Steering risk is one of the easier fair lending risks to control, but it still requires attention. Here are some key takeaways to reduce steering risk in your organization:

- Know and understand all of your product options.
- Write procedures on how product options are offered.
- Give loan applicants a list of product options that includes costs and benefits.
- Understand how loan officers are compensated.
- Perform regular monitoring of lending practices.
- Review your HMDA and product data annually to identify and mitigate risk.

CHAPTER FIVE

Underwriting Risk

LOAN LIFECYCLE

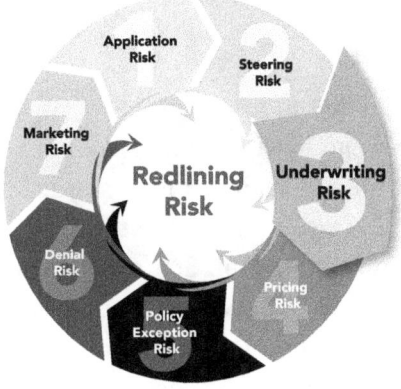

Now that we have taken a loan application and decided what product our customer will receive, it is time for the underwriting process. This is one of the most critical steps in the fair lending loan lifecycle because it determines whether someone will receive a loan.

Before we get too deep in the weeds, let's define a key term: *What is underwriting?*

There is a dictionary definition out there, but here is ours. Underwriting is the process of analyzing a loan applicant's creditworthiness to determine if they can safely repay a loan. While that seems simple and in theory, it is, underwriting has many components.

Let's start with something Tory says and trains on whenever he speaks about fair lending. He even talked about it in *Unfair Lending*, and kicked off his TEDx talk with it:

A lender can legally discriminate against you as a loan applicant.

What? Are you serious? Absolutely.

What we mean by that is there are both legal and illegal ways to discriminate against a loan applicant. In this sense, discrimination simply means treating someone differently than others. When we look at underwriting criteria, those are our legal forms of discrimination. Loan-to-value ratios, repayment ability, and credit score are all common underwriting factors. They tell us whether there will be value left in collateral, whether someone can afford loan payments, and whether they have a history of repaying loans. These factors are legal forms of discrimination that we can and should use to make our loan decisions.

There are also illegal forms of discrimination, and that is where the fair lending laws come into play. The Equal Credit Opportunity Act and Fair Housing Act say we cannot discriminate against someone based on factors like race, color, religion, sex, or national origin. Using these factors in your loan decision violates the law. There are several other prohibited basis factors, but those five are common to both laws.

THE IMPORTANCE OF CLEAR, LEGAL UNDERWRITING STANDARDS

How does a lending institution ensure that its lenders are only using legal factors and never considering illegal factors in loan decisions? It seems like it should be much easier to prevent discrimination than to identify it and fix it after the fact, but how do we do that?

The concept is simple; the discipline to follow through is the challenge.

Clear and concise policies and procedures, consistently followed, are the best way to prevent illegal discrimination in the loan decision process. That means if we write clear guidance for our loan officers and underwriters to follow, and they follow that guidance every time, we greatly reduce our risk. In these cases, everyone has the same opportunity for loan approval.

You may be wondering what clear guidance actually looks like. We have read more loan policies and reviewed more underwriting guidelines than we would ever care to admit, and from time to time, we see things that are obviously unclear.

As we discussed in Chapter 2, we have read loan policies that have stated, "No recent late payments." What does that really mean? Every lender has their own definition of recent.

We talked about a "classic vehicle." Awesome, but what

is a classic vehicle? Someone who is a lifelong Chevy lover may never look at Ford as a classic. Does it need to be a certain age or in a certain condition?

We have also seen "luxury car." Now, what qualifies as a luxury car? Tory always jokes that his 24-year-old daughter thinks a new Honda Accord is a luxury car. Tory loves Hondas and has owned five different Hondas in his lifetime. But in Jon's opinion, a Honda Accord is not a luxury vehicle. What is your opinion? The point is it should not be left to opinion. That is the risk.

We have already said that underwriting factors are your legal forms of discrimination, or the factors you can and should use to make your loan decisions. They ensure your customers receive fair and consistent loan decisions each time, ensure you make safe and sound loans, prevent customers from taking on unaffordable debt, and protect you from fair lending risks tied to prohibited basis characteristics. With all that on the line, it is not too much to ask that underwriting standards be clear, concise, and free from guesswork.

While checking for clarity in your underwriting standards, read them and ask yourself whether the guidance can be interpreted in more than one way. If the answer is yes, you need to try and clarify it. You also want to ensure that you do not have any prohibited basis characteristics tied to your underwriting. That skill takes more thought than just reading for clarity, but it is just as important.

COMMON PITFALLS IN UNDERWRITING

We do not have statistical proof, just experience, but it seems the most common prohibited basis characteristic that tends to sneak its way into underwriting factors is marital status. That does not mean that race or ethnicity are not contributing to discrimination; it has been shown that those factors greatly determine the likelihood of getting a loan. However, what we are trying to say here is that marital status is the most common factor that actually becomes built into underwriting models.

We performed a recent fair lending review, and this bank had some additional guidance written into its income calculation process. Essentially, the guidance said that you could consider additional income that is directly deposited into joint deposit accounts when calculating a debt-to-income ratio and ultimately determining repayment ability. Let's break that down further with an example.

Suppose one of us applies for a loan on our own. We found a brand-new car that we absolutely need to buy. We do not just want the car; we need it. We are sure you know people like that. Our kids *need* things all the time.

Anyway, the loan officer is calculating the debt-to-income ratio and notices additional funds being deposited into our account each month. The loan officer decides to give us credit for that income as well, helping us qualify for the loan. Turns out, those extra funds are our spouse's salary, deposited into the joint account. So, why is this a problem?

Not always, but who is most likely to have a joint account? Married couples. That means this bank is allowing applicants with joint accounts to benefit from their spouse's income, while unmarried applicants do not get that same consideration. In this example, the married applicant is treated more favorably while others will be treated less favorably because they are not married. Marital status is a prohibited basis under the Equal Credit Opportunity Act, so you cannot use that factor against us, or for us, as in this example.

We have also seen several examples of underwriting policies requiring a blanket denial based on the applicant's immigration status. Why is that a problem? Again, we go back to the Equal Credit Opportunity Act, where one of the prohibited basis factors is national origin. If an institution has a policy to deny applicants based on immigration status, that could constitute discrimination based on national origin.

The federal government has issued guidance on this issue, including warnings about blanket denials for anyone without a Social Security number increasing fair lending risk. The core idea of that guidance is institutions must consider all relevant factors when making loan decisions for non-U.S. citizens. Yes, making an unsecured loan to someone on a temporary visa might not be a wise decision. But what about a permanent resident who wants to buy a home? They cannot exactly pick up their collateral and take it with them. The point is to make decisions based on creditworthiness, not assumptions tied to a prohibited basis characteristic. In the last chapter, we will discuss regulatory change, but we wanted to note here that this guidance may likely change again, but the concept behind it remains the same.

THIRD-PARTY RISK MANAGEMENT

We once did a fair lending review for a bank that partnered with several third-party vendors. The partnerships were mostly FinTechs and other financial companies, and these companies would issue credit cards in the bank's name. This kind of partnership is becoming increasingly more common across the industry.

Here is how it worked: the bank brought on a vendor, the vendor created an underwriting model for credit decisions, the bank approved it, and an automated software system made those decisions based on the model. Sounds simple, right? It is, as long as you actually review, approve, and know what is in the model.

We were asked to review this program for fair lending risk. As usual, we put together a document request list and asked for everything we needed to assess risk at each stage of the loan lifecycle. For underwriting, we requested the data input spreadsheet that listed all the underwriting factors because we wanted to know every variable that went into the decisioning model.

The review start date came and went, and we still had not received the underwriting model. We were not concerned yet as we were reviewing several relationships, products, and risks. Another week went by. Still nothing. We followed up and was told, "It is coming." Fast-forward nearly two months later, and we finally received the underwriting model.

Within it, we found a factor that automatically denied applicants whose credit reports showed student loan debt exceeding $25,000. We could not figure out why that would make sense, so we asked the client. They did not know. Wait, what? How could they not know? They reviewed and approved the model before it went live, right? Well, they were supposed to. Student loan debt can be a proxy for age, so it is critical that factors such as this type of specific debt be intentionally used or removed. The problem here was that the client had no idea it was even in the underwriting factors.

We scheduled a meeting with all the key players: compliance, management, third-party relationship managers, and others in the bank involved in this relationship. The bank had been operating under this model for more than 18 months, meaning the FinTech had used it for over a year and a half to make credit decisions on the bank's behalf. When we asked when the bank approved it, things got awkward. After some dodging, finger-pointing, and uncomfortable silence, they finally admitted that the first time anyone at the bank had ever seen the model was when they sent it to us just days earlier.

This was a clear example of poor third-party risk management. Anything a third party does on your behalf; you are responsible for.

The real issue here was that the bank's staff were required to review and approve the underwriting model before it went live, but it never happened. As a result, a questionable factor, student loan debt, was being used as a major decisioning variable for credit card approvals. Why is that such a big deal?

Because who is most likely to have student loan debt? People aged 20 to 30. Sure, plenty of people in their 40s or 50s are still paying off student loans, but the majority of borrowers with large student loan balances are younger, and age is a prohibited basis characteristic under the Equal Credit Opportunity Act. That underwriting factor was effectively using age as a proxy variable, leading to potential age-based discrimination.

We use this example to show the importance of thoroughly reviewing your underwriting policies, procedures, and models. You must understand, in detail, the factors that go into loan decisions and consider whether any group of individuals could be harmed or favored based on those factors. If there is any uncertainty, find a way to clarify it. If there is a less discriminatory way to make decisions, find and consider it.

When we teach fair lending, we always emphasize that clear and concise policies and procedures are the best foundation for a fair lending program but following them is just as critical. You can have a well written underwriting program, but if that program is not followed, it does little to mitigate risk. We will talk more about the importance of following policy in the chapter on policy exceptions.

The Role of Data in Understanding Underwriting Risk

We will round out our discussion of underwriting by talking about data. Knowing your data, and knowing what data to review, is critical to ensuring your program works as designed and that your institution is making fair and consistent loan decisions.

In theory, if you have a solid underwriting program that is free from discrimination and you follow those practices every time, you should never need to review your underwriting data. Why? Because you are always following legal forms of discrimination. While that sounds like a wonderful world to live in, it is not ours. Not every program is that airtight, and not every loan officer or underwriter follows guidance every day. Even the strongest programs can have issues, and people often make mistakes. You need to know how to review your underwriting data.

Before we dig into the data itself, let's talk about two key testing concepts you will need to understand. Most fair lending analyses fall into one of two types of tests: borrower profile or geographic distribution tests.

A borrower profile test focuses entirely on the borrower.

In fair lending, we are interested in the borrower's (or applicant's) personal characteristics such as race, ethnicity, age, gender, or marital status. Depending on the specific test, we may also consider other factors like income for Community Reinvestment Act (CRA) evaluations.

For example, a borrower profile test under the CRA might look at whether a borrower is low- or moderate-income. The test cares about *who* the borrower is, not where they live.

A geographic distribution test, on the other hand, does not care about the borrower's individual characteristics. Instead, it examines *where* the borrower lives. In fair lending, this often means evaluating whether applicants or borrowers live in high-minority areas. Under the CRA, we focus on whether they live in low- or moderate-income census tracts.

Some loan lifecycle tests focus on one of these two types, and some use both.

For example, when evaluating application risk, we should examine both borrower profile and geographic distribution testing results. As compliance professionals, we want to know both where our home loan applications are coming from (geographic distribution) and who is applying (borrower profile). It is 100 percent possible, and unfortunately not too uncommon, to receive applications from high-minority areas at the same rates as your peers, only to find out very few of the applications themselves actually came from a minority applicant. We have seen many times institutions take applications from high- minority areas, but they only receive the applications from non-Hispanic or white individuals in those areas.

If we are looking at steering risk, the focus is mostly on borrower profile. We want to know if minority borrowers are being placed into government-guaranteed loans at higher rates than white borrowers or peers. A geographic distribution test could be helpful. For example, showing if those government-guaranteed loans are concentrated in majority-minority neighborhoods is good information, but borrower profile is the most important test for determining steering risk.

For redlining risk, which we have yet to cover, geographic distribution is the first test you want to consider. It is critical to also review the borrower profile data, but avoiding high-minority areas in lending is the heart of redlining.

Coming back to underwriting risk, borrower profile is where we usually focus. There are three main credit decisions we want to examine: origination rates, denial rates, and fallout rates. We typically will look at these rates for race, ethnicity, and sex; however, we will only use race for the examples below.

Originations are the simplest to analyze. We want to know what our origination rates are by race. To calculate origination rates, take the total number of loans originated to applicants in each race category and divide by the total number of applications from that same category. That gives you the origination rate. Most fair lending software can do this calculation easily. For example, if you receive 100 applications from Black borrowers and originate 60 of those as loans, you have a 60 percent origination rate to Black applicants. Origination rates show the likelihood of approval by race.

Denied applications are just as straightforward. Here, you take the number of denied applications by race and divide by the total number of applications received from that race to find the denial rate. If you received 100 applications, and 20 get denied, you have a denial rate of 20 percent. You can now compare that number to demographic data and more importantly, peer data performance.

The last key data point is fallout applications; those that did not end in a final credit decision. Originated applications were funded, denied applications were turned down, but what about all of the other applications? For some reason, these applicants never reached a final decision. Maybe they withdrew, maybe the application was closed for incompleteness, or maybe they were approved but decided for one reason or another to back out. In short, these borrowers "fell out" of the loan process.

Origination and denial rates are obvious indicators of risk, but fallout rates can be just as critical, often for different reasons. High fallout rates in certain demographic groups can signal reduced service levels or barriers in the application process. For example, if fallout rates among a particular racial or ethnic group are much higher than others, you need to dig into why that is happening.

One of the easiest issues to identify involves language barriers. We once worked with a client whose fallout rate for Hispanic applicants was more than three times higher than for non-Hispanic applicants. Their fallout rate was also more than three times higher than that of peer institutions in the same market. For some reason Hispanic individuals just were not completing the loan process like other individuals, and other institutions in the area had no problem getting Hispanic applicants through the process. What was going on with this institution?

When we asked how many Spanish-speaking employees they had in that area, the light bulbs started going off. There were zero. Many Hispanic applicants simply fell out of the process because they could not communicate effectively with anyone at the bank.

That kind of fallout is not just an operational issue; it

can be a fair lending risk. It is also restricting growth, losing profit, and not serving your community. This institution was taking on risk and losing out on a massive opportunity, all because of an operational challenge flashing a red light in their HMDA data that they never identified.

The last thing to consider is comparative data. Numbers mean little without context. For example, if your denial rate for Black borrowers is 30%, is that good or bad? You need something to compare it to.

The first comparison is to a control group. Typically, the control group is the demographic characteristic least likely to face illegal discrimination or the group with the best performance metrics. In fair lending, white borrowers often serve as the control group for race, non-Hispanic borrowers for ethnicity, and males for sex. That is not a hard and fast rule, but the most common. There are often times that Asian borrowers may have the most advantageous treatment, so they could also be considered a control group.

The group being evaluated, say, Black borrowers, is the target group. If Black borrowers are denied 30% of the time and white borrowers 15% of the time, then Black borrowers are denied twice as often, or a ratio of 2:1. That tells us something important, and regulators pay close attention to those ratios, so you should too.

Comparing target groups to control groups is useful, but it is not always the best indicator of risk. Another key comparison is to peer data, or other institutions in your market receiving similar volumes of applications. Peer comparisons show how your institution performs relative to others, accounting for regional, market, or demographic differences.

Let's say your denial rate for Black borrowers is 30%, while peers' denial rate is 25%. That gives you a 1.2:1 ratio, meaning you're 20% more likely to deny Black borrowers than your peers.

You might wonder why peer comparisons are often better indicators than control-to-target ratios. The answer is not a comforting one as it ties back to the history of discriminatory practices in the United States and their lasting effects on the "on paper" creditworthiness of people of color we discussed in an earlier chapter. While skin color has nothing to do with a person's likelihood of repaying a loan, it does affect critical underwriting factors such as credit score and homeownership rates.

The homeownership gap is actually wider today than it was in 1968, when redlining was still legal. People of color are less likely to own homes, and on-time mortgage payments are a major driver of higher credit scores. Rent payments, on the other hand, rarely count toward improving your credit score. So, if you are more likely to rent, you are more likely to have a lower score.

These realities continue to influence creditworthiness today, and we must acknowledge that when analyzing data. Peer comparisons help account for these structural inequities, by offering a more balanced, market-based perspective.

Knowing that these historic inequities still impact creditworthiness today, at least on paper, we need reliable tools and methods to interpret the data accurately. That is where peer comparisons come in. If your denial rates are in line with your peers, it suggests your performance aligns with the realities of your market, though it does not automatically mean your process is fair. It simply gives you a baseline. If your denial rates are high but in line with peers, it is highly possible that everyone in the market has work to do.

So, the million-dollar question: What denial rate is too high?

Part of the answer comes from statistics. You first need enough data for a fair comparison. Generally, that means at least five applications or loans from your target group and twenty from your control group, though the more data you have, the better. Once you have sufficient data, you can use statistical models to determine whether your findings are statistically significant.

When results are statistically significant, it means the differences you see are not likely due to chance. There is enough evidence to conclude that something real, not random, is causing the disparity. In other words, you can no longer just say, "It is a coincidence." Something in your process may be creating inequitable outcomes, and you need to find out what it is.

We will be honest; neither of us are statistical experts nor will we pretend or even desire to be one. However, having a basic understanding of what statistical significance means is essential. From a compliance standpoint, it is a signal that deserves attention.

For us, when we see ratios above 1.5:1 compared to peers, that is when we start to perk up and take a closer look. That means you are doing something 50% more often than peers, such as denying certain applicants; however, the ratio of 1.5:1 is just a starting point. We have seen ratios of 1.3:1 be major issues when considering the number of files or impacted customers we are considering. The more applications, originations, or credit decisions in the sample, the more critical a smaller ratio can become.

The universe size, or the number of applications or loans in your sample, matters greatly. If you have a 75% denial rate but only four applications, that is too small of a universe to draw any meaningful conclusions. Denying three of four applicants tells you little statistically. However, if your denial rate is 75% on 100 applications, that is a different story. At that point, you likely have plenty of data to warrant a deeper look, which usually means a file analysis.

The good news is that most fair lending software programs will calculate statistical significance for you. But even then, do not rely on it completely. It is just one tool in your toolbox. Statistical tests are not perfect, and they do not tell you definitively whether you have a problem; they simply point you toward areas worth investigating.

You can also conduct geographic distribution tests for denial and fallout rates. If possible, look at your denial and fallout rates in high-minority census tracts. This is where underwriting risk begins to overlap with redlining.

When a disproportionate number of denials occur in majority-minority areas, you may be looking at more than just underwriting issues, you could be seeing potential redlining patterns. If individuals in those areas consistently cannot get approved for loans, the impact goes beyond underwriting fairness and into the realm of access to credit and community reinvestment obligations.

REDUCING UNDERWRITING RISK

Understanding underwriting risk is not just about reading ratios or reviewing files. It is about connecting the dots between data, policy, and human behavior. Every underwriting decision reflects your institution's values, whether you intend it to or not.

With clearly written policies and procedures that are consistently followed, underwriting risk becomes a very manageable part of the loan lifecycle. But clarity and consistency are nonnegotiable.

KEY TAKEAWAYS

- Thoroughly review all underwriting guidance and question anything that can be interpreted in more than one way.
- Ensure your guidance is never tied to any prohibited basis group.
- Regularly review origination, denial, and fallout rates using borrower profile and geographic distribution tests.
- Compare your performance not just to control groups but also to peers in your market.
- Investigate any areas with higher ratios or statistically significant disparities and if necessary, conduct a file review.
- Consider how other parts of the loan lifecycle, like product offerings and marketing, might influence underwriting outcomes.

CHAPTER SIX

Pricing Risk

LOAN LIFECYCLE

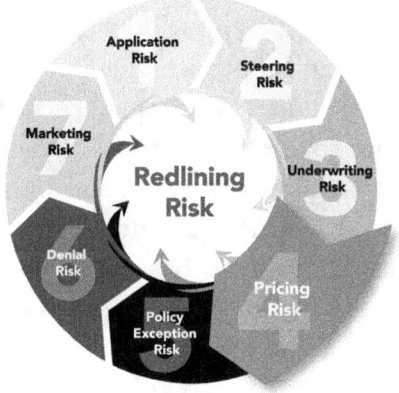

After the underwriting decision, the applications that are approved and originated must move on to the next risk - Pricing Risk.

When we think about pricing, the most obvious factor that comes to mind is the interest rate. The rate is critical because it determines how much interest someone will pay over the life of the loan. Interest rates are numerical values, meaning they are not subjective like some underwriting factors and can be easily compared across different loan recipients. But the interest rate is not the only pricing factor we need to worry about.

Fees can also be a major component of pricing, especially in mortgage lending where charges can add up quickly. This is where the annual percentage rate (APR) comes in handy. While the interest rate represents the simple interest you pay over the life of the loan, the APR incorporates additional finance charge fees and annualizes them over the loan's term.

The Truth in Lending Act, implemented by Regulation Z, defines finance charges and the APR. Regulation Z is not a traditional fair lending regulation, and we will not be going into how to calculate the APR here. If you are a seasoned compliance professional who has calculated APRs, you already know the frustration. If you are newer to compliance, we will not spoil the fun for you. The point here is that fees can significantly increase the cost of a loan, and the APR can often be a better metric for assessing pricing risk.

Loan terms are also tied directly into pricing risk. Most interest rate pricing policies, often referred to as rate sheets, tie the interest rate to the loan term, especially in consumer lending such as auto loans. For example, one axis of the rate sheet (perhaps the rows) may list the age of the collateral, while the other axis (the columns) lists credit scores and loan terms.

Basic credit principles tell us that the greater the risk, the shorter the loan term should be. If you have a brand-new car, you may feel comfortable offering a seven-year loan term because the car still has a long useful life. However, you would not want to give someone a seven-year loan on a ten-year-old car. That car will be 17 years old by the end of the term! As such, you might only offer three years for the term of the loan.

Someone's credit score is also a common factor driving loan term decisions. You face much lower risk offering a long loan term to a highly creditworthy borrower because they have a well-established history of repaying loans. Someone with a very low score, on the other hand, might not be someone you want to offer long repayment terms.

Because loan terms and rates are often tied together, loan terms become part of pricing risk. That means loan terms are a factor, although not always a major one, and one that you may want to consider in your analysis.

THE IMPORTANCE OF CLEAR PRICING STANDARDS

Building a strong pricing model that is free from discrimination follows the same concept as building a strong underwriting model: Clear and concise policies and procedures, consistently followed, is the best way to reduce pricing risk.

In the context of pricing risk, it means giving your lenders a rate sheet that is clear, easy to follow, and used on every loan. Just like underwriting guidance, well-written pricing guidance represents your legal forms of discrimination. If someone presents a higher risk of not repaying their loan, you can charge them more to compensate for that risk. That is legal discrimination. Clear guidance that is consistently followed greatly reduces that risk.

In the underwriting chapter, we talked about vague guidance such as "classic car" or "luxury car." Those same vague categories show up in pricing guidance as well. Each type of loan product should have its own pricing guidance, but it must be crystal clear which loan types fall into which category. Let's look at an example.

Say an institution has a rate sheet labeled "Car Loans" and another rate sheet labeled "Other Secured Consumer Loans." What types of collateralized loans fall into each bucket? If we were guessing, we would likely say that all normal cars and trucks fall into the first bucket. But what about recreational vehicles? Are they considered a car loan or an other-secured loan? What about a boat, jet ski, or a trailer?

If loan officers do not know, they will guess. That means some loan officers will put these gray area loans into the car loan pricing bucket while others put them into the other secured bucket. And by the way, the other secured bucket usually carries much higher rates than a typical car loan.

Now imagine one loan officer who always puts these gray area loans in the higher-priced bucket works in a high-minority area, while another loan officer who always uses the lower-priced bucket mostly serves white applicants. Suddenly, you begin to see major pricing disparities based on race or ethnicity, even though the intention was not discriminatory.

A better way is to define loan buckets clearly is to list out every collateral type that falls into each category. Some institutions use the term "vehicle-titled loans." This is more specific because it implies that the borrower must title the vehicle and obtain a license plate. But then we have to ask, does this cover vehicles like ATVs or lawn mowers that may not require titles?

These are basic but extremely common examples of rate sheet ambiguity that we see every day. The solution is simple: Be specific, be deliberate, and clarify exactly how each loan type should be priced. The goal is to ensure every market, every branch, and every loan officer always uses the right rate sheet, no matter the loan type or collateral taken.

GEOGRAPHIC PRICING

We get this question monthly: "We have one market that is incredibly competitive. Can we lower our rates in that market only?" Yes. You can. If you have a market where your rates simply are not competitive and you refuse to lower them, you might as well shut down that location because it will not survive. However, pricing differently across markets comes with challenges.

Let's say you have two markets separated by 100 miles. We will call them Market A, which is a highly competitive metro market, and Market B, which is rural with very little competition. You want a lower pricing rate sheet for Market A because competition demands it.

But what happens when someone from Market B travels to Market A to buy a car? Market A, being a major metro area, has more dealerships and more choices, so this is not uncommon. Do they get the Market A rate or the Market B rate? That is the challenge.

If you give them the lower Market A rate, but their neighbors who shop locally get the higher Market B rate, and you do this often enough, you may begin to see pricing disparities. If one prohibited basis group disproportionately engages in this behavior, such as men, your data may indicate that women are paying higher rates.

Most institutions resolve this by pricing loans based on the market where the customer lives (or will live, in the case of home purchase loans), not where they shop. With the customer's address, institutions can quote accurate rates based on the market where the borrower normally conducts business. This approach makes the most sense for banks and credit unions with branch networks and defined geographical footprints. Non-deposit institutions and mortgage companies may not face this issue as strongly.

Look at national institutions' websites. Smaller, single-market institutions will post rates directly. But nationwide banks usually ask for your zip code before quoting a rate. They do this to ensure their rates are competitive for that specific market, but also to reduce fair lending risk by pricing consistently within each market.

Another critical component of reducing pricing risk follows the exact same methodology as underwriting risk: ensure lenders are actually following policies and procedures.

By the end of this book, we will sound like a broken record, "Strong policies and procedures, consistently followed, is the best way to reduce fair lending risk." We repeat this over and over because it is that simple and that important.

If you develop underwriting factors, your legal forms of discrimination, following them is how you avoid using illegal factors like race in your credit decision. The same is true in pricing. Having pricing guidance, such as a rate sheet that is clear and concise and used every time, is the best way to ensure institutions are not pricing based on prohibited factors such as race or sex.

Some organizations, although they are in the minority, never allow pricing exceptions. You take their rate or you go to the institution down the street. These organizations have the lowest pricing risk, but they will also lose business as a tradeoff. Other organizations hand out pricing exceptions like candy on Halloween. These organizations have the highest potential pricing risk as a result. We will talk about both underwriting and pricing exception risk in the next chapter.

USING DATA TO ASSESS PRICING RISK

Now it is time to review your data. Regulators and auditors have a lot of tools available when it comes to assessing pricing risk.

One of the most common is the gender and surname tool. This tool uses decades of census data to determine the likelihood that a first name is male or female, and a last name is Hispanic. These tools are not perfect, and our modern understanding of gender is much different than it once was. We are not making assumptions to disrespect or offend anyone. We are using a tool to help determine whether an institution is treating people fairly and consistently with the data available. If you also have HMDA data, you can add race, marital status, or age to your analysis.

Once you choose which prohibited basis characteristic to review, break your data into a control group and a target group. The general rule is that the control group is the group least likely to face illegal discrimination, and the target group is the prohibited basis group most likely to face illegal discrimination for which you want to test.

Starting with the prohibited basis of sex, the control group is any loan where a male is present. This includes a single male borrower, two male borrowers, or a male and female jointly. The target group is any loan with only female borrowers. This is typically a single female, but sometimes you might see two or more female borrowers.

Once you have your control and target groups, calculate the average interest rate, by product, for each group. Subtract one group's average rate from the other group's average rate to get your rate disparity. Most pricing analyses focus on the simple interest rate, but if you have the APR, you could use that as well.

For example:
- Control group average: 7.62%
- Target group average: 7.96%
- Rate spread (rate disparity) = 34 basis points

Now comes the million-dollar question: Is that good or bad?

The answer: yes, no, we do not know, and it depends all at once. We realize that is not helpful, so let's try and break it down.

First, you must look at the universe size, or the number of total loans in your review, to determine the statistical significance. If you have a 34-basis point disparity but only four loans to the target group, we are not really concerned. That is not enough data to form meaningful conclusions. But if you have 1,000 loans in the target group? Now we are on to something. In that case, the data shows women are paying one-third of a percent more than men and the data is statistically significant. Now, we need to understand why.

One of the most common reasons we see pricing disparities by sex is the coborrower problem. Regulators will usually break down control and target groups based on borrower presence as we have described, but this might not always be the best or fairest way to assess pricing performance. Coborrowers may sometimes skew your analysis in a way that disproportionately and unfairly favors the control group, or in the case of sex, the male group.

If, and only if, your pricing model uses the higher of the credit scores to set rates with joint borrowers, then you may want to go a step further. If your pricing model does not use the higher score method, do not apply this extra step.

Many institutions will price based on the higher of multiple borrowers' credit scores, and there is nothing wrong with that. But this pricing method tends to favor the control group because many control group loans involve married couples buying a car or home together. This means you often have more borrowers in the control group for each loan than the target group.

If it is a male and a female on the loan, the loan will be considered in the control group because of the male presence. If you force distribute credit scores, and many of the control group loans have a male and female borrower, it means roughly half the time the female has the higher score, thus lowering the interest rate.

However, target group loans are often a female only borrower, so they do not commonly get the benefit of an extra borrower with a potentially higher credit score to lower the rate. As a result, control group loans often have lower average rates and target group loans look unfairly priced even when lenders followed the policy. Fortunately, there is a way to correct this.

Do not throw away your original analysis. Keep it and show it in your report, but now we are going to do a second analysis with no coborrowers. To do this, you simply throw out all loans that have more than one borrower, so all you have left is loans to single individuals.

Once you do this, find the average rate for single males and compare that to the average rate for single females for that particular loan product. If the disparity drops significantly, perhaps close to zero, you can reasonably conclude that coborrowers caused the disparity. If the disparity to the target or female group stays high, you likely have a pricing issue that will take more research.

When it comes to doing a pricing analysis on ethnicity, your control group is loans with only non-Hispanic borrowers. Your target group would be loans where any of the borrowers are Hispanic.

For race, you would put loans with white only borrowers in the control group. The target group would be a loan where any of the borrowers are a minority race, or you can focus just on one race at a time.

Our pricing reviews often start with the institution's loan download, typically a one-year history of all originated loans exported to Excel. This file can usually be pulled from loan software, and then we break down the loans by product based on how they are priced. Consumer-purpose loans are typically the focus of our pricing reviews. Though with 1071 data, we will be able to do this analysis on commercial loans as well.

We conduct dozens of pricing reviews every year, so we see this data constantly. We have seen over 100 basis point spreads to the target group, but with low loan volume, it may not yet be an issue. On the other hand, a 50-basis point spread with hundreds or thousands of loans can be highly significant.

To perform a meaningful pricing analysis, you must understand your pricing models and practices and group similarly priced loans together. For example, if you price all one-to-four family residential real estate loans the same way, group them together for analysis. But many institutions price secondary market loans differently, and in that case, separate them into another product category. Adjustable-rate loans or construction loans are also often priced differently and should be broken out into their own categories as well.

For smaller institutions, once you break your data down that far, you may not have many loans left in each product universe. That's okay. It simply means you do not originate many loans in that product category, so your overall pricing risk is lower. You should still run the numbers to see your performance, but know that with small volumes, one outlier can significantly skew your results.

Once you see your rate spreads for each product, if you identify high spreads, you can further break down your analysis by market, branch, or even individual loan officers. We have seen an institution that had one market price car loans to female borrowers 250 basis points higher than to male borrowers. Another institution priced unsecured loans 700 basis points higher to women. A third institution priced auto loans 100 basis points higher for Hispanic borrowers. When you find rate spreads this high, it is time to dig into the data and conduct interviews to find the root cause. This also often requires a file analysis to verify whether lenders correctly followed the rate sheet.

One final thought on pricing reviews; always start with the prohibited basis of sex, especially for non-real estate loans where race or ethnicity data is unavailable. This factor is the best starting point because roughly half the population is male and the other half is female. This means we naturally have a good distribution with a near 50–50 distribution of male and female borrowers. This gives you larger universe sizes, which means better statistical reliability and more meaningful comparisons.

Conversely, many rural institutions may not have enough data to conduct meaningful race or ethnicity analyses because the minority percentage of the population is too low. Furthermore, there are tools such as the Census Bureau's gender tool that make it possible to perform a meaningful analysis even when you do not have HMDA demographic information.

A pricing analysis based on sex that reveals low rate spreads on all products is a good indicator that loan officers understand and are consistently following pricing guidance. That does not mean you do not have issues in areas such as race or ethnicity, but it is a valuable starting point to assess if loan officers know, understand, and follow policy.

Performing simple, routine pricing analyses is one of the best ways to verify your program is functioning as intended. However, pricing reviews are not "one and done." They are a continual check-in, an early warning system for your fair lending program. Conducting these pricing analyses year after year provides valuable trend data and tells a powerful story of whether your fair lending risks are improving, worsening, or holding steady.

For example, consistently low or shrinking disparities suggest your team understands and follows the pricing guidance. Alternatively, emerging disparities may signal a change in institution behavior, market dynamics, or clarity of the guidance. Likewise, persistent disparities point toward deeper structural issues, including unclear rate sheets, inconsistent training, or potential discrimination. These trends help you prioritize where to investigate and where to adjust policy or training.

REAL WORLD EXAMPLE

Sometimes pricing issues are unintentionally built directly into the rate sheet. We conducted a fair lending analysis for an institution whose pricing guidance instructed lenders to use the lower credit score if joint borrowers lived together and use the higher credit score if joint borrowers did not live together. Yes, you read that right. What problems does this model present?

This disproportionately harmed married individuals. If you apply for a car loan for your family with your spouse, you get priced based on the lower credit score. But if you apply for a car loan for your business with your sibling who does not live with you, you get priced based on the higher score. We were stunned when we read this guidance, and we even told the client this would be an example we would use in a book to show what not to do. It was not a lie; here we are.

When we asked why this policy existed, the institution's reasoning was at least based on underwriting principles. They said married couples are likely to share debt, so using the lower score felt like a better reflection of risk. But regardless of the intent, the procedure tied the pricing decision to marital status, which is a prohibited basis characteristic.

As mentioned in the underwriting chapter, marital status is often the prohibited basis characteristic that finds its way into an institution's policy or procedures, and this is yet another example of that. That does not mean that race or gender are not critically important or play major roles in credit decisions, but they are just not implicitly written into policy, intentionally or not, like marital status often is.

The takeaway is clear guidance, consistently followed, is the start of a strong pricing program. Your pricing model should be carefully designed; free from ambiguous or subjective language; used consistently across all lenders, branches, and markets; and reviewed regularly for disparities. Then performing simple reviews on prohibited basis characteristics, using the control and target group methodology, is a simple way to verify your program is working as designed.

Pricing risk, very much like underwriting risk, is entirely manageable when you build a structure that supports fairness and follow it every time. When pricing is handled correctly, it protects your customers, your institution, and your entire fair lending program.

Key Takeaways

Pricing is one of the most sensitive and highly analyzed areas of fair lending. When disparities occur, they impact borrowers every month for years, sometimes decades. Small errors, inconsistencies, or vague policy language can lead to big problems.

Your fair lending program becomes exponentially stronger when you:

• Establish clear, detailed pricing guidance.

• Define specific product buckets.

• Create consistent market-based pricing rules.

• Document expectations for rate exceptions.

• Conduct annual or more frequent pricing data reviews.

• Have a willingness to investigate and correct problems quickly.

Pricing risk is highly manageable, but only when approached with clarity, consistency, and discipline.

CHAPTER SEVEN

Policy Exception Risk

LOAN LIFECYCLE

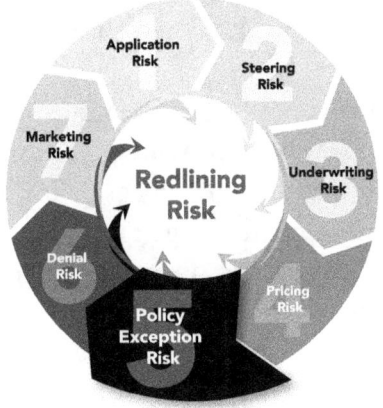

It has been a few pages since we have said this, so it is due: **Strong policies and procedures, consistently followed, are one of the best ways to reduce fair lending risk.**

Alright, we will not keep saying it (maybe), but we wanted to kick off this chapter with that thought because it leads us directly into the policy exception risk portion of the loan lifecycle.

Think of it this way. If you write clear loan decision guidance that is free from discrimination, and your lenders follow it every time, you can almost eliminate most of your fair lending risk. While that is a wonderful thought, and it would make the jobs of compliance and auditing professionals significantly easier, it is just not the world we live in.

WHY POLICY EXCEPTIONS EXIST

Not everyone fits neatly into the same box. Some applicants may have a lower credit score but strong income and repayment ability that helps compensate for the risk. Other applicants may have saved a large down payment, lowering their loan-to-value ratio, but are borderline on the debt-to-income requirement.

These are common examples of underwriting exceptions. While an applicant may not perfectly meet all underwriting requirements, they may excel in certain areas that help offset where they fall short. Perhaps they are a long-time customer of the bank and have demonstrated their willingness to repay your loans. If only we had a quarter for every time we heard a loan officer say "Well, they may not always pay all of their bills on time, but they always pay me back first." Some of you reading this may be laughing right now because you have heard it as well. If you are a lender reading this, it is possible you have said it.

On the pricing side, the most common exception to policy is lowering the interest rate to match competition. A potential customer can get a better rate down the street, so they want to know if you will match it. There are many other reasons to grant a pricing exception, but that is the most common one we hear.

Whenever a lender or underwriter approves a loan, or gives a rate outside of approved guidance, a policy exception is created. Policy exceptions themselves are not inherently bad. They can help customers get loans they otherwise would not qualify for; however, when internal controls are weak, exceptions can quickly balloon into a major fair lending issue.

Tory has been on all sides of the compliance table, and his views have shifted over time. He started as a federal bank examiner, then moved to an internal bank auditor role, then a compliance officer, and now works as an external consultant. His perspective on policy exceptions has evolved throughout his career. Jon has also served in very similar roles, so now he has had the chance to see this shift as well.

Starting as an examiner, and learning banking from that perspective, Tory thought that everything a lender does outside of approved policy is scary, and therefore, wrong. Examiners view decisions solely from a compliance and fair lending risk standpoint; they do not consider organizational growth or profit. Approving a loan outside of policy is dangerous, and you may ask yourself why on earth would you ever want to do that?

When Tory became a banker, he began seeing things through the banker's lens. If you grant a policy exception, you can meet a customer's needs. You may have personal experience with that borrower and know they always pay back your institution. That perspective makes policy exceptions feel more reasonable.

Now, as a consultant and business owner, he cares about his customers, his employees, and maintaining profit to keep the business moving forward. Turning away customers because their risk profile is slightly outside approved policy does not always make business sense anymore.

UNDERSTANDING POLICY EXCEPTION RISK

So, what is the real risk with making policy exceptions?

There are really two angles to tackle this problem. Let's first look at the safety and soundness angle.

Your organization's leadership, whether that be executive management or the board, sets standards and policy for making credit decisions. Your loan policy, paired with underwriting standards, determines the amount of risk your organization is willing to take when making a loan.

That means any loan approved outside of the established criteria is riskier than what the organization formally adopted as acceptable. If you continually make loans with exceptions, you may have higher repayment risk, increased likelihood of defaults, and higher losses for your organization.

These principles do not just apply to mortgage or consumer lending, but all lending aspects, even commercial or small business lending. Too many underwriting exceptions can jeopardize the safe and sound nature of your institution. For those of you that work with risk management examiners, you know they get excited when your risk goes up, and not in a good way.

There is the risk management angle, and there is the compliance angle to exceptions. Policy exceptions are a major compliance and fair lending concern because there is risk that exceptions are not approved on a fair and equitable basis but on a prohibited basis characteristic. This is the heart of this chapter and the policy exception risk as it relates to fair lending.

We have seen too many times where it is not deliberate, but an organization always seems to make exceptions to men, not women; white borrowers, but not minority borrowers; or the geographic distribution analysis shows exceptions seem to be concentrated in white neighborhoods, not high-minority neighborhoods. With enough exceptions and no controls, this is often what ultimately happens.

We feel the best way to illustrate policy exception risk is with a case study. This is an actual institution in which we helped identify issues and build a stronger fair lending program.

The story begins with a standard annual pricing review. We broke down the institution's loan download into product categories and calculated the average rate they offered to male and female borrowers for car loans. Because this was a large consumer institution, they had a significant volume of auto loans and plenty of data to analyze. Pricing based on sex looked pretty good. Rate spreads were reasonable, and earlier we told you borrower sex is a great place to start, but it does not tell you the whole story.

This institution served pockets of high Hispanic populations throughout their market, so we decided to use the surname tool to conduct a pricing analysis by ethnicity. What we found was very different from the sex-based analysis. In fact, Hispanic borrowers were paying, on average, 125 basis points more for a car loan than non-Hispanic borrowers. Since we had several hundred loans in our sample, we knew the dataset was large enough that we had to dig much deeper.

The first place we like to look to is policy exceptions. We wanted to see whether the bank was granting pricing exceptions to Hispanic borrowers. The problem? They did not track exceptions at all. They had no idea how often rate exceptions were granted or who was receiving them. With a 125-basis point spread in a large dataset, we recommended that they start tracking exceptions. They agreed and started tracking. Then, we waited.

A year later, we returned to conduct our next annual fair lending review. They did not change anything with how they did business, but they did implement exception tracking data. When we analyzed car loan pricing based on ethnicity, we saw the exact same trend: Hispanic borrowers were paying roughly 125 basis points more for a car loan than non-Hispanic borrowers. But this year, we had all important pricing exception data.

What we found is that this institution approved 70 total exceptions in that past year for interest rates, and 69 of those 70 rate exceptions were to non-Hispanic borrowers. That means that while Hispanic borrowers originated hundreds of loans, only one got a rate exception.

We now have multiple years in a row with very unflattering pricing results, proof that Hispanic borrowers are not getting rate exceptions (for at least one year), and the picture is now becoming clearer. There is a ton of fair lending risk, and the policy exception process is likely the root cause.

This does not happen often, but right in the middle of our exit meeting with the client, the CEO spoke up and said the bank was done with rate exceptions. Effective immediately, no more pricing exceptions because he did not want to continue taking on the unnecessary risk. And they stopped, just like that.

They asked us to retest pricing in six months rather than wait a full year, so we did. Six months later, we compared the average rate given to Hispanic borrowers versus non-Hispanic borrowers for car loans. The disparity, which had been around 125 basis points for two years, dropped to just 2 basis points. That's right; two basis points. Essentially, the disparity was now completely gone. We had found and eliminated the root cause that Hispanic borrowers were simply not receiving rate exceptions, but the story does not end there.

As part of nearly every fair lending audit we conduct, we also do a fair lending interview. A fair lending interview is where an auditor, or examiner, or it could be you as a compliance professional, sits down with a lender and asks them basic questions on how they do their job. Prior to the interview, the interviewer must prepare by reading policies and procedures, knowing underwriting guidance, understanding how pricing works, and likely knowing how the exception approval process should go. In other words, you need to have a basic understanding of how lenders are supposed to do their jobs.

Then, you sit down, ask basic questions, and play dumb for 30 minutes. You ask questions such as:
- "How does the application process work?" (application risk)
- "How do you determine what products to offer customers?" (steering risk)
- "Walk me through your underwriting process and what criteria you consider." (underwriting risk)
- "How do you set interest rates or other pricing factors?" (pricing risk)
- "Are you allowed to deviate from loan policy?" (policy exception risk)

We typically ask a few questions per risk category, but the

point of this exercise is the answers you get from your lenders should match what you have read in policies and procedures. In other words, you are simply verifying that the lenders know, understand, and follow the approved lending program. Fair lending interviews are one of the most critical tools for a compliance officer or auditor conducting a fair lending interview, but they are one of the most underutilized.

During our review of this institution's fair lending program, we did a fair lending interview. By just pure chance, we happened to interview one of the two Spanish-speaking lenders they had, and she was a consumer lender.

Once we got to the policy exception process, we asked basic questions about how she gets exceptions approved. Once we discussed pricing exceptions, we finally reached the core issue. She always followed the rate sheet. Always. She never requested a rate exception. And turns out, neither did the other Spanish-speaking loan officer.

Is that wrong?

No, it is not inherently wrong to not ask for rate exceptions. These lenders always followed policy. They wanted to do their jobs the right way, and they did not want to take additional risks, so they always followed policy. We have seen many lenders on the exact opposite end of that risk spectrum and ask for policy exceptions on every loan. Those lenders take the most risk, but these two lenders always wanted to do it by the book. That is not a problem, but the institution's overall culture of granting policy exceptions was.

As you likely guessed, nearly all Hispanic borrowers were funneled to these two lenders because they spoke Spanish. Since they never asked for rate exceptions, Hispanic borrowers were always priced following the rate sheet. Since the other loan officers worked with non-Hispanic borrowers, and they had no problems asking for rate exceptions, non-Hispanic borrowers were constantly approved at rates below the rate sheet requirements while Hispanic borrowers were not. Not any one particular loan officer was doing anything wrong. It was the lack of control of the process and having no idea what lenders were doing that led to this problem.

While it took some time to find the root cause, we eventually got there. We could have identified the root cause on day one had the institution tracked exceptions. Since these reviews and revelations, the institution went back to approving rate exceptions, but they are a lot more conservative in the process. They now only approve exceptions in certain cases, track all exceptions, and do continual analyses of the process to make sure it is fair and equitable.

This example again helps illustrate how the different parts of the loan lifecycle interact with each other. Weak oversight and a poor policy exception approval process was leading to excessive pricing risk. Not tracking policy exceptions kept the risk hidden, so nobody had any idea on the problem's root cause. Sometimes when you identify problems in one area, you may need to look at other areas to solve the problem.

What Does a Good Policy Exception Program Look Like?

It starts with the policy exception approval process. Your organization needs a way to approve policy exceptions quickly but fairly. That begins with establishing the right approval structure. You should have a small group of highly trained individuals, ideally senior lending staff, approving all policy exceptions.

We have seen too many times where every branch manager or even every loan officer's supervisor is allowed to approve exceptions. This rarely works out in an institution's favor because often there is no overarching guidance on the approval process or no standardized training for loan staff, so every supervisor is approving exceptions in a vacuum based on their own experience. That means you will have some supervisors that approve exceptions constantly while others never do, just like you have some lenders that request exceptions all the time while others do not.

Once you look at the customers and geographic areas those supervisors oversee, you can easily imagine how quickly this can become a problem. Returning to our earlier example, if the supervisor of the two Spanish-speaking lenders was extremely conservative and never approved exceptions, while other supervisors frequently did, you immediately get inequitable results, even though none of it is intentional. The risk does not stem from the loan officers; it stems from poor planning and oversight. You eliminate most of that risk by ensuring that only a few senior lending staff approve exceptions.

It is also not wise to have only one exception approval authority because that person will not always be available, and bottlenecks create operational delays. However, the more decentralized the approval process is, the more potential risk your program will carry. The safest approach sits in the middle with a small pool of well-trained approvers with clear authority and who apply policy consistently.

The next step, after establishing how exceptions are approved, is to establish how they are tracked. To perform a meaningful analysis, you need good data.

In the pricing chapter we talked at length about how to set up your target and control groups. To do that, you need both the borrower's and coborrower's information. To find both genders and surnames, you need first and last names.

Too often, we see exception logs missing the most critical pieces of information, especially coborrower data. Why is gathering all of that data important?

Let's illustrate using the prohibited basis of sex and say the exceptions tracking log only includes the main borrower's name. If the main borrower is a male, it is easy. You know it is a control group exception, regardless of who the coborrowers are. However, if the main borrower is a female, it could be a control or target group exception. If a woman is the main borrower, and her husband is on the loan, but you do not include his information on the exception log, that policy exception will be coded as a target group when it should actually be in the control group.

The same thing goes for race or ethnicity. If the main borrower is white or non-Hispanic, you really do not know if it is a control or target group because that will be decided by the coborrowers information, which is not included in the data.

When coborrower information is missing, exceptions may get incorrectly coded as a target group exception when it should have been in the control group. This skews your testing results. Collect first and last name of the borrower and all coborrowers on your exceptions tracking log. It is the only way you truly know if they are control or target group exceptions.

How to Analyze Your Exception Data

Once you have solid data, your goal is to determine whether exceptions are granted fairly and equitably. There are two main approaches to attack this.

The first approach is to compare your exceptions data to

your originations data. For example, if you looked at car loans in your pricing review, and you found that 30 percent of your car loans originated to Hispanic borrowers, what percent of exceptions do you think should be granted to Hispanic borrowers? Is 25 percent or 32 percent acceptable? Likely, yes. But if 30 percent of loans went to Hispanic borrowers and they only received 3 percent of exceptions, you are 10:1 behind on your ratio, and it now becomes an issue to research.

The second approach is to calculate the exception rate for the control and target groups. Take the number of exceptions to each group divided by the total number of loans to each group and see how those numbers compare. For example, let's say you made 20 exceptions out of 100 loans to the control group. Your exception rate to the control group is 20 percent. During the same period, you made 5 exceptions out of 50 loans to the target group. The target group exception rate is 10 percent. In this case, control group individuals are twice as likely to get an exception as target group individuals for a 2:1 ratio.

Regardless of the way you cut up your data, the end goal is the same. You need to determine if someone is more or less likely to receive an exception based on a prohibited basis characteristic like sex, ethnicity, or race.

While much of this chapter focuses on pricing exceptions, underwriting exceptions follow the same logic. Whenever an underwriting exception is approved, track it the same way you track pricing exceptions. You also want to track what underwriting criterion was the source of the exception. For example, if you made a credit score exception, that is your exception reason. If you have more than one exception reason, list them all.

Just like with pricing, you will want to know that your underwriting exceptions are being made fairly and equitably to all prohibited basis group individuals. Underwriting exceptions also serves that dual purpose of risk management **and** compliance/fair lending, and sometimes the risk management reason is the only reason why some institutions are currently tracking exceptions.

Tracking underwriting exceptions serves as a fair lending risk mitigation tool, but it also has safety and soundness/risk management value. When a loan defaults, one of the first places to look at is the policy exceptions to see if that loan was approved with an exception. We have found that for many institutions, this is the only reason they track exceptions, purely for safety and soundness, while the fair lending purpose is overlooked.

The Misplaced Focus on "Why" Exceptions Happen

Before wrapping up this chapter, we want to address one last key point, and it is often at the center of many questions we receive on this topic. Compliance and audit professionals frequently focus on the "why" behind exceptions. For example, we are often asked, "If we grant a pricing exception, do we need to keep an actual quote from the competing institution in the file?" These professionals get so wrapped up in documenting and proving why an exception was made that they miss the much bigger picture.

Yes, it is good to document the why. It is also good practice to show proof of the exception. It shows a stronger program, but in the end, does the why really matter from a fair lending perspective?

Not as much as you think.

Let's look at the old argument we have heard for years: men tend to shop for rates and women do not. You could also go back to our client example and say that those non-Hispanic borrowers asked for rate exceptions and the Hispanic borrowers did not. Even if those statements were true, and often, they are only based on assumptions, do they change the end result?

It might help explain the root cause of the problem, but in both cases, men or non-Hispanic borrowers are still getting the much lower average rate, and those are both prohibited basis characteristics and likely violations of the law. Stop focusing so much on proving why an exception was made. Instead, focus on the results of those whys because in the end, that is what really matters.

The entire point of opportunity in lending is to ensure that everyone gets the same opportunity each time, and that includes an underwriting exception to get a loan approved or a better rate, regardless of the reason. If certain individuals, groups, or neighborhoods are not receiving the same opportunity, then the why really does not matter (except to maybe identify the root cause for corrective action). The results of the program and those decisions are what is key.

KEY TAKEAWAYS

- A strong approval process is the foundation. Ensure you have solid controls on approving exceptions and an appropriate number of trained approval authorities.

- Minimizing the number of exceptions overall is one of the easiest ways to reduce risk in this area.

- Good data is essential. Without complete and accurate borrower and coborrower information, it is difficult to perform meaningful analyses.

- Analyze your exception tracking data and be willing to recommend changes to the process when there are inequitable results.

- Focus on the testing results, not just the reasons behind exceptions. The outcomes, not the explanations, determine fairness.

CHAPTER EIGHT

Denial Risk

LOAN LIFECYCLE

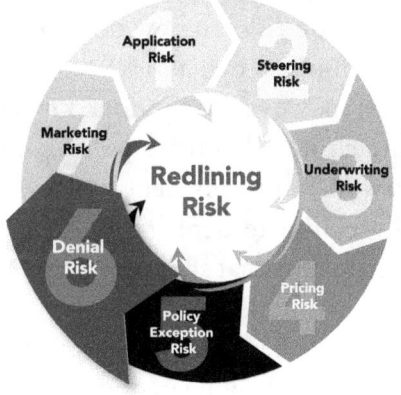

If you have been paying attention so far, you might be thinking that denial risk is really part of underwriting risk. That is somewhat true. The underwriting decision can end in different ways, and a denial is one of those ways. If a loan is approved, it moves on to other risks such as pricing and redlining. If the loan application is denied, it moves on to potential denial risk.

So, what is denial risk? Our definition is the risk that loans are denied at a disproportionate rate to prohibited basis group individuals. You can also look at it as loans that should have been approved but were denied, or loans that should have been denied but were approved.

We spent a lot of time talking about numbers in the underwriting chapter: denial rates, ratios comparing your performance to peers, and other metrics that help identify increased credit decision risk. So how do you build a program that reduces or eliminates denial risk?

We do not think we have mentioned it yet in this book, but if you write clear and concise policies and procedures, free from guesswork, and consistently follow them, you can almost virtually eliminate denial risk. Broken records, we know, but nowhere does that show up more often or become more important than in denial risk.

Let's say you have been paying attention, and you have gone through all of your policies and procedures for making credit decisions with a fine-tooth comb. Then what? You monitor your denial data. HMDA data and good software is a simple way to do that, but there are other things you can do as well.

CMS Monitoring - Denial Risk

One of the best ways to strengthen your CMS and fair lending program is through secondary reviews of denials. These reviews are part of your CMS program monitoring and can be as simple or as robust as your risk profile requires. When it comes to your CMS, many of the elements are straightforward. Policies and procedures are often written down, you train your people and document through training records, and audits usually end with a report. But monitoring, the ongoing, real-time check, is often the least formal and least documented part of a program.

Secondary reviews of denials are a great way to show your examiners that you have a hands-on approach to your fair lending program, and it is much quicker and more timely feedback than waiting on an annual audit to identify issues.

What is the most common form of denial monitoring we see?

For the smallest institutions, usually a second set of eyes will review the application and denial documents to see if they agree with the credit decision. More robust programs will have a compliance analyst review to ensure the adverse action notice is correct and the denial reasons are accurate. The strongest programs do a thorough review of the denial file and track that data for further analysis.

Too often, however, we see institutions with no secondary review of denied files at all.

Unlike annual audits, which look back on a prior period's decisions, timely secondary reviews examine current credit decisions. Ones that literally happened possibly even the same day. When you do an audit and there are issues, there is nothing you can do to go back and fix them. It is still great information to improve your program going forward, but those decisions have been made, and those applicants are long gone. Sometimes in a fair lending audit of denied files, you may be looking at credit decisions made one to two years prior.

On the contrary, with the frequent and timely secondary reviews that we call CMS monitoring, you can make real-time course corrections if there are errors. Regulation B says we have 30 days to communicate a credit decision, so you do not need to deny the file that very moment and send the notice out the door. On your obvious approvals and denials, fine. Make the credit decision right then and there. But for borderline applications, especially those that may require underwriting exceptions, take the time to complete a secondary review or get a second opinion.

This brings us to our next topic, something very new at the time of this writing, though if you are reading this many years later, it may be old news.

FAIR LENDING-AS-A-SERVICE (FLAAS)

You may be asking yourself, what the heck is FlaaS? If you do not know, do not feel embarrassed or too out of the loop. When Tory was asked to speak about this topic on the Fair Lending Colloquium main stage, he casually mentioned backstage to the moderator, moments before going on, that he still did not fully understand it. It actually made for good banter on stage by joking that a panelist was learning about the topic as it was being discussed.

Here is what we believe FlaaS to be: FlaaS consists of software tools that provide real-time feedback on credit decisions. Imagine a powerful data computation and AI tool that knows your underwriting standards, all of your past credit decisions, and your basic borrower characteristics. Now imagine you are about to deny an applicant with a 635 credit score, but the FlaaS program knows that your institution has approved 6 people in the last week with a 630-credit score and flags the decision. Real-time feedback helps prevent fair lending issues before they happen; however, this concept does not come without drawbacks.

FlaaS tools are just that, tools. They are not meant to be used for underwriting, so just because it tells you that you are doing something out of the ordinary does not mean you should always change your credit decision. If that were the case, then it is essentially making the underwriting decision for you.

FlaaS tools are models, and with that requires some model validation. AI is not necessarily smarter than humans. It is better at processing large datasets and identifying patterns and anomalies quickly, something humans can do, but significantly slower and with greater risk of error. Think of AI as a higher form of automation. Ensuring your FlaaS tools and models are working as necessary is critical before you rely on them to improve your process.

At the time of publication, there are not many companies in this space. However, in 10 years, it may be a way of life for institutions. Time will tell, but we all know AI is expanding, and this is just another tool and method of that expansion.

TRANSACTION TESTING

As you build out your fair lending monitoring program and expand how you perform secondary reviews of denials, the accuracy of your credit decisions should also be a main focus. This may seem obvious, but it is not always the case in practice.

Whenever we perform fair lending audits for clients, we always transaction test a sample of denied applications and review the adverse action notices. Yes, we are looking for technical issues. The denial reasons must be accurate, there are timing requirements, and when a credit bureau and score are used, additional requirements need to be on the notice.

However, we also evaluate the underwriting decision itself. It is not uncommon to see a denial for "income," only to find a 25 percent debt-to-income ratio in the file. For those unfamiliar with underwriting, that is a pretty solid ratio. For most home loans, you can go up to 43 percent or more. In that denied file, the loan officer or underwriter simply got it wrong or made a documentation error. Maybe the loan would have been denied anyway for delinquent payments but denying for income when the applicant clearly met your underwriting income requirements is a problem, and it is the kind of problem that secondary reviews can easily catch. FlaaS could also help automate that process.

Remember, if you deny an application and do not review the file until two months later, you are past your 30-day window, and that customer is long gone. You cannot simply call them back and make them that loan. The car they wanted to buy or the home they hoped to purchase is most likely no longer available. If you find these issues in a timely secondary review, there is still time to correct these mistakes.

Low Denial Rates

Let's rewind for a moment and revisit denial rates more broadly. We talked in detail about denial rates in underwriting. High denial rates to certain prohibited basis groups, especially when worse than peers, are key risk indicators. But what about low denial rates? Extremely low denial rates also tell a story. Earlier, in the application risk chapter, we talked about screening applicants. If you make 1,000 loans and deny only 4 applications, that tells you something. In that earlier example, we indicated that screening could be contributing to low denial rates.

We have a client that fell into this exact category. Tory performed their first fair lending review, and their HMDA denial rates were between 1–2 percent. We could not believe it. How could they be denying only 1 or 2 out of every 100 applicants? It did not seem logical, so we turned to peer data.

Peer data is critical because it helps you understand what the market is doing. If all institutions in your area have extremely low denial rates, it may indicate a very prosperous market, though that is highly unlikely. Here, peer institutions had HMDA denial rates between 15 and 40 percent. Clearly, something was off with our client's operations, and we suspected screening. We mentioned all of this to the client, we recommended that they do some training, and that was the end of it. They did not provide any further details.

Fast forward to the next annual review, and Jon is the lead consultant. Again, denial rates were 1–2 percent, but during a fair lending interview with a residential real estate lender, Jon learned about their extensive and voluminous pre-qualification process. Bingo. Now we are starting to get to the root cause of the problem.

Formal *pre-approval* programs must be reported under HMDA. However, most institutions do not offer them, mainly because of that reporting requirement. However, _pre-qualifications_ are different. The underwriting is much less in-depth, and those easy to identify denials likely never get reported.

For example, let's say a borrower comes in wanting to be pre-qualified for a home loan as they want to purchase their first home. Their credit score is 500. That file will get denied immediately, but because they do not have a property identified, it is not HMDA-reportable. That means it never shows up in the HMDA dataset. If enough pre-qualifications are denied before reaching the application stage, your HMDA denial rate may appear extremely low.

Does that mean your fair lending risk is lower? Of course not. It just means your institution likely has to take the extra step and analyze pre-qualification denials because they do not show up in your HMDA data.

This is yet another example of how the loan lifecycle works together. In this case, the application process led to data anomalies which skewed underwriting and denial data, all of which was uncovered through a fair lending interview. It is also an illustration of why you cannot just buy fair lending software and believe everything it tells you. Software and data are a great starting point, but they are only tools, and their main job is to point you in the direction of where to go next. There is often more to the story, and good compliance and audit professionals learn over time where to go next.

COMPARATIVE FILE REVIEWS

Let's wrap up this chapter with a discussion on conducting comparative file analyses. If you have never had the pleasure of performing a comparative file review, you are truly missing out. It is such an enjoyable task, one that never frustrates the reviewer and always tells the full story. And if you believe that... we also have a bridge for sale in New York City.

Comparative file analyses can be a painstaking process that requires a tremendous amount of time and effort. And as you perform them, you often find new issues and anomalies forcing you down additional rabbit holes to explain results. Sounds fun, right?

While we collectively have been part of hundreds of fair lending exams and audits, very few of them actually required a file analysis. The ironic thing is that when we talk to most compliance and audit professionals, the first thing, and often the only thing they do for fair lending audits, is a file analysis. But that really should be the last step in the process. A file analysis is only warranted when you find anomalies in your data that cannot be explained by any other means.

WHAT IS A COMPARATIVE FILE ANALYSIS?

A comparative file analysis is the process of reviewing borderline loan approvals and denials to ensure borrowers were treated fairly across prohibited basis groups. The best way to explain this is through an example.

Let's say your underwriting data review shows that one prohibited basis group has denial rates three times higher than peers. You have reviewed policies and procedures, interviewed loan staff, examined the policy exception process... and still found no explanation. This is when a file analysis becomes warranted.

Step 1: Identify the Worst Approved Loan

Start with one underwriting factor. In this example, let's choose credit scores. You review all loans for a specific product during your review period and identify the worst credit score that was approved. Let's say that score is 600. This becomes your lower baseline.

Step 2: Identify the Best Denied Application

Next, flip through all denials for that same product and year. Anytime you see a denial for credit score, pull it aside. Your goal is to identify the best score that was denied. Let's say the highest denied score you find is 650. This becomes your upper baseline.

Step 3: Establish the Sample Range

Everyone denied for that product with a credit score between 600 and 650 becomes your sample. Let's say there are five total denied applications in that range. That means you found five instances where someone had a credit score better than 600, your worst approved, but their application was denied. These five files become your focus.

Step 4: Compare All Other Underwriting Factors

Now compare the other underwriting criteria to see whether the decisions make sense. Let's assume our approved borrower, with a score of 600, had a loan-to-value ratio of 70 percent and a debt-to-income ratio of 30 percent. Both of those are likely well within approval range. Now compare that to the denied borrowers in the 600–650 range. Maybe you discover that the denied applicants have loan-to-value ratios over 100 percent or debt-to-income ratios over 60 percent.

These are the mitigating factors that explain why a lower

score borrower was approved while higher score borrowers were denied. This is exactly what a file analysis is designed to uncover.

PRO TIP:
START WITH POLICY EXCEPTIONS

Your policy exceptions are a great place to find borderline approvals. Why? Because if an underwriting exception was granted, it is likely the borrower was approved with weaker creditworthiness than someone who was denied without an exception. These are the perfect starting points for file comparisons.

If this sounds like a lot of work, that is because it is. We are still haunted by memories of file analyses we completed years ago. Reviews can take several weeks to conduct as they can consist of hundreds of files, every anomaly requires a follow-up, and every factor has to be documented. This is why a file analysis is the last resort. It is a lot of work, and you can often find the root cause of issues before that point, if you know where to look.

That is one of the goals of this book. To be a well-rounded compliance and audit professional, you must have a deep understanding of all fair lending risks and how they relate to one another.

Many large, multi-billion-dollar institutions perform file analyses as part of their regular fair lending audits. That is not surprising, with thousands of loans, anomalies are common. Usually, they rely on software that can automate the file analysis, and that is great. If you have software that can find anomalies in your HMDA data with the click of a button, there is no reason not to take advantage of it. But compliance professionals at a smaller institution may go an entire career without ever needing a full file analysis. There is nothing wrong with that either.

The best way to avoid ever needing a file analysis in the first place is through a strong program. That means well-written policies and procedures, strong controls over the exception process, and secondary reviews of denied credit decisions.

REDUCING DENIAL RISK

Fair lending is fundamentally about opportunity and prevention. Give everyone the same opportunity to move through the loan lifecycle and build a program that prevents issues before they occur, and you are going to have a good time. It is much easier to manage risk by eliminating it from occurring early than by receiving fair lending reports filled with issues and not knowing where to even start.

KEY TAKEAWAYS

- Have a secondary review process for denials.
- Consider tools, such as FlaaS, to assist you in monitoring credit decisions.
- High denial rates are indicators of potential risk, but extremely low denial rates also tell a story and should be investigated.
- File analysis is the end of the fair lending review process when no other explanation remains, not the starting point.

Marketing Risk

LOAN LIFECYCLE

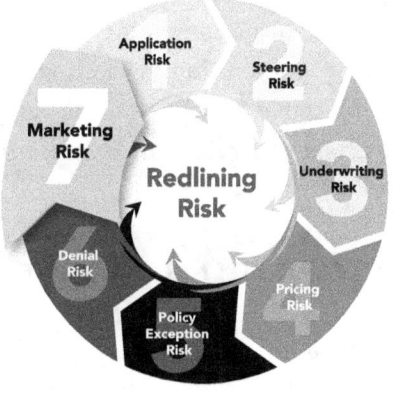

We have finally made it to the last piece of the loan lifecycle outer circle: marketing risk. You could easily argue that marketing risk actually kicks off the loan lifecycle. A customer may hear your advertisement on the radio or television, visit your website, or see signs or billboards as they drive to your physical locations. Perhaps you do targeted online marketing or social media marketing.

The reason we put marketing at the end of the loan lifecycle is because we believe it is important to understand all of the other loan lifecycle risks first before discussing marketing risks. Marketing risk is unique because it is the one risk that, by itself, can significantly increase or decrease your overall fair lending risk. When marketing is done effectively, it can have a major impact on application rates or redlining risk, which we will discuss in the next chapter. When marketing is done poorly, or not at all, it can amplify those risks.

In simple terms, fair lending marketing risk is created by the commercial messages you put out about your organization, your products and services, or your brand.

BRAND IMAGING MARKETING

Smaller financial institutions tend to focus on brand imaging marketing. They do not often talk about particular products or services and rarely mention interest rates. This approach is generally safer from a consumer compliance perspective because it reduces the need for additional disclosures that are required when advertising specific products or rates. When you stay away from product specifics, you also reduce the risk of being unfair or deceptive in your messages.

Brand imaging marketing is about telling the public what

type of organization you are or where your values are focused. Some institutions position themselves as "your premier hometown bank" or your "local credit union." Others position themselves as a mortgage lender or small business lender. The idea is to sell your vision, not necessarily your products.

We have always viewed brand imaging marketing as lower compliance risk, and it is, but we are no longer as convinced that it necessarily results in lower fair lending risk. If you are struggling in other fair lending risk areas, particularly application risk or redlining risk, brand imaging may not be the solution. For example, if you are not receiving applications from high-minority neighborhoods and minority individuals specifically, selling a generic brand message is unlikely to bring those customers in. In those situations, you may need to launch a specific marketing campaign to have any real impact.

While the overall goal of marketing in any industry is to drive brand awareness and attract customers, the goal for financial institutions is to do that while also reducing fair lending risk. To accomplish that, you need to understand **how, where, and to whom** you are marketing.

The How: Understanding Your Marketing Channels

The first step is understanding how your organization markets its products and services. There are many traditional and non-traditional marketing channels, and the best place to start is with your marketing team. If you are a very small institution, marketing may be handled by one person, or it may even be an additional duty for someone with another primary role. As institutions grow, we often see entire teams dedicated to marketing. Regardless of where you fall on that spectrum, someone in your organization should know the "how" when asked to explain how you market products and services.

The simplest way to find this information is to interview your marketing team. We do this in nearly every fair lending audit we conduct, and it is something you should be doing as well.

Marketing has changed significantly over the years. In the 1900s, newspapers were one of the most common ways to advertise. If you are not familiar with newspapers, they are essentially the internet printed on paper and are outdated almost immediately. Financial institutions once had large newspaper budgets because newspapers dominated the news cycles. The internet has changed this quite dramatically.

Radio was also a major outlet for marketing, particularly in smaller rural communities. While many people still consume music, much less of that consumption happens through traditional radio. With streaming services now the norm, institutions may need to engage customers in different ways.

Of course, television continues to be a way to market, but how people consume visual media has also changed dramatically. At one point, there were only a handful of television channels. Tory still remembers being the youngest of four, also known as the family's "remote control". When it was time to change the channel, Tory walked to the TV to do it. It was a simpler time for media, for sure.

Today, there are seemingly unlimited ways to stream content. Mass media channels like radio and television broadcast messages broadly, making them expensive ways to reach audiences. Targeted media platforms, such as streaming services, allow institutions to be more deliberate about how messages are delivered.

Billboards are still fairly common, especially in major metropolitan areas. They can be effective at grabbing attention, but they do not move. In other words, if billboards are placed only in certain neighborhoods, only those residents will see the advertisements. Too often, we talk with marketing teams that have zero clue the demographic makeup of the neighborhoods where their billboards are located. When they sit down to map them, they sometimes find those billboards are disproportionately located away from higher-minority areas.

You can put your brand on almost anything today. Local banks and credit unions sponsor local sports venues, with logos displayed on scoreboards or outfield walls. Some of the largest institutions even have their names on professional sports stadiums. In small rural communities, we still see sponsorships and logos on the local café menus.

These traditional methods still have a place, but the growth of the internet and smartphone technology has transformed marketing. Today, social media dominates much of the marketing landscape.

Social media is a great and often cost-effective way to get your brand in front of potential customers. There are many different social media sites, and if we list them here, this book will likely be easily dated in no time. We still remember one of the original social media pages – Myspace. What a throwback that seems at this point.

Social media allows for paid advertising, retargeting ads for people who have visited your website, and continued brand exposure across digital platforms. Paid online marketing can also include search advertising, with Google being one of the most common outlets. When someone in your geographic footprint searches for relevant keywords, you will show up as an option, albeit maybe just a paid ad.

Organic search visibility is often the most effective way to attract traffic. That means your page is clicked on enough where you organically show up as a top search option. Achieving this requires consistent engagement and website traffic over time.

There are many other "hows" when it comes to marketing financial products and services, but these represent the most common channels we see in the lending industry.

The Where: Knowing Where You Market (And Where You Don't)

Once you understand how your organization markets its products and services, the next thing you need to understand is specifically where your message is being sent. The "where" you market is just as important as the "where you are not" marketing.

Some marketing channels make this fairly easy. If you advertise on local television or radio stations, you generally know the reach of those outlets. The same goes for newspapers and magazines. If you purchase billboard space, someone should know exactly where that billboard is located.

Online marketing, however, is different. With digital advertising, institutions often have the ability to control who sees their message, when they see it, and where they see it. That flexibility creates opportunity, but it also creates risk.

If you have the budget to run a nationwide television advertising campaign, you have very little control over who sees your message. Anyone watching that channel at that time will see it. That is the best way to describe mass media. You put your message out to the masses, and they consume it with you having very little control over who sees that message.

Mass media is an effective way to get your message in front of a large audience (think Super Bowl commercials), but many of those people will never become customers. Take our business as an example. We are a small consulting firm that is specific to bank compliance. We are often asked to sponsor events where our company and logo will be displayed in front of thousands of people. Is that an effective use of marketing dollars for a niche business-to-business consulting firm?

If we sponsor a local event, how many of the attendees do you think run a bank or credit union, specifically looking for consumer regulatory and fair lending compliance services? If you laughed or even smiled a bit when reading that, you had the appropriate response. Hardly anyone. That is mass media in action - you are going to get your message out in front of a lot of people that will never be your customers.

Targeted marketing allows you to choose who sees your message. When done effectively, it delivers more value for your marketing spend by focusing on actual potential customers.

Home equity line of credit (HELOC) marketing is a great example of this. Let's say you want to market HELOCs, so maybe you are going to send out a mailer either to your customers or potential customers. Do you think you should send that message to everyone? That could get expensive and wasteful. To qualify for a HELOC, a borrower must own a home with available equity. If you have a list of homeowners, you could target marketing efforts to those individuals instead of to a student who only has a checking account.

Targeted marketing seems like a great idea, and it is, but execution is what potentially gets financial institutions into trouble. Once personal characteristics are introduced into the decisioning factors, we can quickly increase our fair lending risk. That is because we possibly start crossing prohibited basis boundaries, which we cannot use in any aspect of the credit decision.

Let's stay with the HELOC example for a moment. If you decide that people under the age of 25 are unlikely to own homes and remove them from your marketing list, you have now used age as a factor in determining who sees your marketing materials.

We see similar risks in student lending. Jon was part of a fair lending review of a financial institution that had a student loan program. During interviews with staff, they mentioned they specifically marketed to the areas surrounding universities and only to individuals between the ages of 18 and 25. They were clearly using age as a decisioning factor. Many people carry student loan debt into their 40s, and it is increasingly common for grandparents to sign student loans for their grandchildren. Additionally, there are many individuals who choose to go to college later in their careers. Yet they were limiting their marketing by age, which is a prohibited basis characteristic.

The heart of the "where" part of the marketing equation is knowing the geography where you are marketing and where you are NOT marketing. When organizations target marketing efforts into low-minority areas and intentionally or unintentionally choose to avoid high-minority areas, you will start to see the effects of redlining, and marketing will likely be a major contributing factor.

We once received a call from a concerned compliance officer. She was very knowledgeable about both fair lending and her institution's performance. See, her bank was struggling to lend in the one section of high-minority geographies in her bank's assessment area. They have always performed poorly there when it came to taking applications and then ultimately making loans in this area. She knew they had high redlining risk.

They had attempted marketing in those neighborhoods by sending mailers and putting up billboards, but none of those efforts were effective. Management eventually concluded they were "wasting their money marketing there," and the bank ultimately stopped marketing in the high-minority neighborhoods altogether. Let's walk through how this would play out during an examination.

If we were the examiners, we would analyze HMDA data and see almost no originations in those high-minority neighborhoods. That would be the first red flag. We could also map originations on a minority map, and a horseshoe around the high-minority areas would likely be there.

Next, we would look for application risk and see if they are even receiving applications from these high-minority areas. Of course, we would show almost no applications received from the region. By the way, if you receive applications at the same rate in an area as your peers but originate significantly fewer loans, your redlining problem is likely triggered by something else. Either your underwriting team is dropping the ball, or perhaps you need products that are better suited to the market so people can get approved. In our case, both origination rates and application rates were well behind peers.

We would then examine the bank's branching structure

and see that the bank had no branches near the high-minority neighborhoods. Mapping branches over a minority map, like with our originations and applications, would also be a nice appendix for the redlining case against them.

Finally, we would review marketing efforts. A simple conversation with the marketing team would reveal that the bank had made no effort to market to members of this community. All of these facts added together is the information we would need to start our redlining case against this bank.

If the bank had continued marketing in those areas, devoted resources to relationship building, and worked with community members, regulators would likely allow time for improvement. When regulators are forced to intervene, that is often when we see formal fair lending cases emerge.

Understanding where you are marketing and where you are not marketing is a critical part of your overall fair lending risk profile. This is like your geographic distribution test.

The Who: Understanding Who You Are Marketing To

Since we have already talked about this quite a bit, we do not need to go into too much additional detail, but who you are marketing to is the last critical piece of the puzzle. This is like your borrower profile test. This can be learned based on the how and where.

If you know how you are marketing, you should have a good understanding of your intended audience. If you know where you are marketing, you should also know the general demographic makeup of the people who live or operate in those areas.

The "who" is critical because your lending activity should be somewhat representative of your communities. In other words, if 30 percent of your community consists of Hispanic individuals, then, all else being equal, your lending to Hispanic individuals should be somewhere near that percentage. However, if 30 percent of your market is Hispanic, but only 3 percent of your loans are made to Hispanic borrowers, you have significant potential fair lending risk. In that scenario, Hispanic individuals are represented in your market at ten times the rate they are represented in your lending.

This is the big difference between a borrower profile and geographic distribution test. The borrower profile is the who, and the geographical distribution is the where. Both are critical to know, and we will take a deeper dive into both in the next chapter.

KNOWING THE NUMBERS

It is critical to know your application and origination rate numbers because they are key risk indicators. If you are 5 to 10 times behind lending to a particular category of people in your area, you need to know that so you can consider real-locating resources, such as marketing efforts. However, it is important to make sure you are doing so for the right reasons.

We once had an institution call us and explain that they had an upcoming examination and needed four Hispanic applications in one specific neighborhood. That was literally how the phone call began. The institution kept focusing on the number four and that one particular area. As consultants, it is our job to look at the bigger picture and help institutions build strong, sustainable fair lending programs. As such, we tried asking broader questions about their strategy and performance, but the conversation continued to circle back to the number four. "We need four applications in this one area" they kept saying.

Eventually, we stopped the conversation and just asked, "why do you need four Hispanic applications in this one neighborhood?" He simply blurted out "because that will make my disparity go away." That was an eye-opening moment. This made us realize that not everyone wants to solve fair lending problems for the same reasons.

Based on the institution's performance, their fair lending software had identified a disparity and calculated that four additional applications in this particular area would remove the red flag. That is good information to know, but that is also all that he cared about; making a red flag go away.

Let's step back and look at the bigger picture. He did not care about growing his organization, helping the members of his community thrive, or seeing the local neighborhoods improve. All he cared about was one number on a report. We did not partner with this lender or his organization, so I do not know how this all turned out for him. Had he taken the approach that they could expand their efforts into this community and watch both the neighborhoods and his organization grow and prosper together, he would never have to worry about numbers in a report again.

GEOFENCING

With advances in technology and the expansion of internet banking and smartphone capabilities, institutions now have the ability to market using sophisticated digital tools.

One of those tools is geofencing.

Geofencing essentially allows an institution to place a virtual pin on a map and instruct marketing platforms, such as Google or social media networks, to deliver advertisements to anyone located within a defined radius of that pin. Essentially, a virtual circle is drawn on a map, and anyone within that circle becomes part of the marketing audience. Geofencing is not a new concept, but it seems many financial institutions do not fully understand the associated fair lending risks.

In many cases, geofencing can actually reduce fair lending risk. Most institutions geofence around their physical branch locations, which makes sense. People who live or work near those locations are more likely to do business with the institution. So, when does geofencing become a problem?

If your physical branch locations are concentrated only in low-minority areas, geofencing around those locations means you are marketing exclusively to those populations. In turn, your customer base will reflect that limited audience, and you will begin to see poor performance across application rates, origination rates, and redlining metrics.

A simple but powerful exercise is to ask your marketing team whether they are using geofencing and then map those virtual boundaries over a minority census map. This exercise is often eye-opening and can significantly change how institutions view their marketing and fair lending risk.

THIRD-PARTY MARKETING

If you work for a financial institution, your organization should be good at one thing: offering financial products and services to customers. Regardless of your size and resources, this is pretty much a requirement for you to be good at, or business will be quite difficult.

As institutions grow, so do their budgets and capabilities. Many organizations, both large and small, choose to outsource some or all their marketing efforts to a third party that is good at helping organizations tell stories and sell those products and services.

It is okay to outsource marketing efforts. Just like you need to be good at offering great financial products and services, marketing firms need to be good at selling their clients' products and services. So, where is the risk?

If you are a seasoned compliance professional, you already know this principle, but let's say it out loud for those that may be newer to the game. Basic third-party risk principles clearly state that you are liable for everything a third party does on your behalf. That means any product, service, or marketing message you pay someone to build, offer, or sell for you, it is your organization that holds the risk and liability.

Marketing firms are often excellent at crafting compelling messages. What they are typically not experts in are the dozens of federal consumer protection laws and regulations that govern financial institutions. That is where good oversight of your process is key, and that cannot be outsourced.

If you work with a marketing firm that often partners with other organizations like yours, they likely will better understand the complexities of the regulations we manage daily. If they are new to the financial industry, they may have little or no understanding of the restrictions and scrutiny involved. It is critical that institutions educate their marketing partners on what is permitted in the financial services industry, and that all marketing efforts are monitored closely.

We have seen too many times where a client allowed marketing firms to have free reign over the marketing message and efforts, and this rarely ends well. Use third-party marketing as a powerful tool, or a force multiplier, that works with you and your CMS. But do not let them operate independently as they often do not understand the regulatory requirements and scrutiny we face in our industry.

KEY TAKEAWAYS

- Brand imaging marketing may reduce compliance risk but does not necessarily reduce fair lending risk.

- Institutions must understand how, where, and to whom they are marketing (borrower profile and geographic distribution).

- Targeted marketing can be effective but introduces risk when personal characteristics are used.

- Where an institution does not market can be just as important as where it does.

- Marketing efforts should align with community demographics and lending performance.

- Geofencing can reduce risk when used thoughtfully but can embed discrimination when branch locations lack diversity.

- Institutions are fully responsible for third-party marketing activities and messaging.

CHAPTER TEN

Redlining Risk

LOAN LIFECYCLE

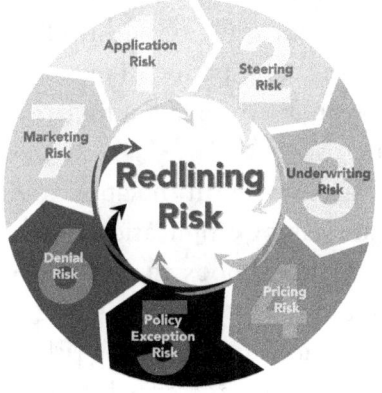

Redlining is when a lending organization does not make loans into particular geographic areas, and spoiler alert, they are high-minority areas. It is very much a geographic distribution-based test used to determine whether an institution is avoiding areas with high-minority populations. You can Google the textbook definition, but in its simplest terms, redlining is avoiding neighborhoods and areas of cities based on population demographics.

If you look at the loan lifecycle graphic that opens most of the chapters in this book, you will notice there are several steps in the circle. Generally, a loan applicant will go through these steps. They submit an application, get steered into a product, go through underwriting and pricing, some will receive a policy exception, others will get denied, and many of them will see marketing. Where does redlining fit?

Redlining does not really fit within the loan lifecycle itself. Instead, it is the culmination of one or more fair lending risks. In other words, any fair lending risk can ultimately lead to redlining risk.

Redlining can show up in the application process when organizations are taking applications much less often in high-minority neighborhoods than peers or demographics suggest they should.

Redlining can show up in steering risk when residents of high-minority areas are targeted with government-guaranteed loans when they qualify for conventional loans or are targeted with less advantageous products that have higher rates, higher fees, or shorter terms.

Redlining can show up in underwriting or denial risk when minority borrowers experience higher denial or fallout rates because of where they live.

Redlining can show up in pricing risk when minority

individuals or high-minority areas are disproportionately receiving higher rates or paying higher fees than white borrowers or low-minority neighborhoods.

Redlining can show up in policy exception risk when
minority areas and minority individuals are significantly less
likely to be approved for a loan with an underwriting exception or receive a lower rate to match competition.

Redlining can show up in marketing risk when high-minority areas are eliminated from marketing efforts and resources.

Any or all of the loan lifecycle risks can contribute to
redlining risk. They are all interconnected, but one lifecycle
risk may be a significant contributing factor, or all may be
contributing factors. It is up to a knowledgeable compliance
or audit professional to put the facts and data together to
find the root cause.

Of all fair lending risks, redlining is the most devastating
to communities. When neighborhoods are denied access to
credit, they suffer, remain stagnant, or plunge into genera-
tional poverty. In Tory's TEDx talk, he discusses the racial
wealth and homeownership gaps and explains how not only
they are not closing, but they are getting wider.

Redlining was officially made illegal in the 1960s, yet the
homeownership gap is actually wider today than it was when
the practice was still legal. How is that possible? It is due to
institutions that, while maybe not always intentionally, continue to avoid putting resources into minority areas.

In 2021, the federal government launched the Combating Redlining Initiative. The goal was to bring together different federal agencies, along with state partners, to reduce
or eliminate redlining in the United States. The government
successfully brought and prosecuted several redlining cases,
but the change in administration in 2024 caused these ef-

forts to come to a screeching halt.

Even prior to the Combating Redlining Initiative, we had seen many cases dating back to the turn of the century. We have read most of these cases, and the peculiar thing is they often seem like carbon copies of one another. While a few cases are somewhat unique, they share many common characteristics.

BRANCHING STRUCTURE

From a historical perspective, branching structure was one of the dominant causes of redlining. Financial institutions would open branches only in predominantly white neighborhoods, and these branching structures would often create circles around high-minority areas. If you go back and review settled redlining cases from the 21st century, many include images of branch locations overlaid on minority population maps showing this problem.

As technology evolves and more people bank almost entirely online, branching structure may not be quite as critical. Nonetheless, having a physical presence in a community remains one of the best ways to reach and serve its residents. Today, we also see several financial institutions that are completely online. As that trend continues, this factor may carry less weight in the future.

MARKETING EFFORTS

Where any business chooses to market its products or services has a major impact on its customer base. If an organization predominantly markets in certain areas while simultaneously avoiding others, they will predominately get customers from the marketing concentrated areas. This has a major impact on the institution's footprint and the make-up of their clientele.

As discussed in the marketing risk chapter, marketing efforts, messages, and resources are directly linked to redlining risk. It is not hard to imagine that you will not see many customers from high-minority neighborhoods if you never market to them.

Product Options

Not having the right products to meet the needs of your market can also lead to redlining risk. As mentioned earlier, we worked with a client that had high denial rates and offered zero government-guaranteed loan options. This led to deficiencies in their program and heightened redlining risk.

Your product offerings must make sense to the areas in which you operate. If customers cannot qualify for loans because the products you offer do not meet their needs, you are not only increasing your redlining risk, but you are missing opportunities to grow.

Loan Officers

This trend is more recent in the history of redlining cases, but it is just as critical. We have seen several redlining cases where institutions had branches in or near high-minority areas, so branching structure was not an issue, but there were no loan officers in those branches.

Having a branch in a neighborhood you seek to serve

gives you a big leg up on the competition, but what is the point if there are no loan officers there to originate loans? No lending staff to serve the customers in the area is something we have been seeing. While this seems obvious, it happens much more often than you would think.

COMMUNITY CONNECTIONS

There is often deep mistrust of financial institutions in minority communities due to the history of redlining in the United States. Many neighborhoods remain unbanked or underbanked not only because of limited branches, products, or marketing, but because of historical mistrust in the system.

We attend many banking and lending conferences each year, some focus specifically on fair lending, and experts consistently agree that establishing strong community connections is one of the best ways to rebuild trust and form meaningful relationships with residents in the areas you intend to serve.

If there was one piece of advice we would give to any financial institution struggling with redlining or looking to expand into underserved communities, it would be to identify key stakeholders and start building relationships. Once you get your foot in the door, build trust, and show you are there to lend, you can experience growth and prosperity that no branch or advertisement will ever be able to reach.

USING DATA TO IDENTIFY REDLINING RISK

Looking at your organization, you may see some of the issues we have talked about. It is not difficult to map branch locations, speak with marketing staff, look at your loan officer organizational chart, or assess community involvement. However, there is another powerful tool for identifying redlining risk that we have referenced throughout this book: data. Community Reinvestment Act (CRA) data is a good starting point, and consumer and commercial loan data can be helpful, but there is no better place to begin a redlining analysis than HMDA data.

As discussed previously, there are several ways to analyze this data. You can compare your performance to census demographics or peer institutions, and you can perform both borrower profile and geographic distribution analyses.

One good place to start is by evaluating whether your lending reflects the population demographics of your market. While software simplifies this process, it is not required. Publicly available census data can show the demographic makeup of an area, and HMDA data can show how your lending aligns with that information.

We have discussed how if 30 percent of your community consists of Hispanic residents, it would be reasonable to expect that your level of lending is commensurate with the demographic makeup of your area and also consists of around 30 percent Hispanic borrowers. If your performance shows only 3 percent of loans originated were to Hispanic borrowers, you are lagging the demographics by a ratio of 10:1.

Following the same approach, you should understand how your peer institutions perform. Remember, your peers are other banks, credit unions, and mortgage companies in your area that have similar resources and volume of your institution. If peers originate 30 percent of their loans to Hispanic borrowers and your institution originates only 10 percent, you are behind peers by a ratio of 3:1. It is important to note that redlining cases have settled at ratios equal to or less than this.

You can repeat this analysis for any prohibited basis group using both demographic and peer data. Exact alignment is not required, but once your ratios exceed approximately 2:1 behind your benchmark data, it is time to act.

If we have these two different data sets (census demographic and peer data), which one is more important? Well, they are both important, but sometimes it makes sense to favor one over the other. To illustrate this point, let's use CRA performance standards. We realize that not all institutions are subject to CRA performance evaluations but hear us out.

CRA analyses focus on income-based testing rather than race-based testing. When reviewing an institution's performance, CRA evaluates lending to low- and moderate-income (LMI) individuals and compares that performance to both census data and peer institutions. In other words, we can see if a bank's lending matches the number of LMI people in an area and what peers are lending to those same people. However, one will always give us drastically skewed numbers over the other in this scenario.

If census data shows that 10 percent of an area's population is low-income individuals, an institution will likely never originate 10 percent of all HMDA loans to low-income borrowers. There is a simple, plausible, and legal explanation for this. Most low-income people have a reduced capacity to borrow and will not qualify for home loan financing, so it is nearly impossible to reach that 10 percent threshold.

Let's say we are reviewing an institution's performance, and they originated only 3 percent of their loans to low-income borrowers when the population says they make up 10 percent of all residents. That means they are more than three times behind population demographics. That must be bad, right? That will get criticized, right? Not really. Since low-income people often cannot qualify for loans, census data is not the best threshold to measure. That is where peer data comes in. When we look at peers in that same market, let's say on average they lend four percent of all home mortgage loans to low-income borrowers. That means we are only slightly behind peers if we are at three percent. The reason why it makes more sense to compare to peer data in the case of income is peers are a better representation of the market conditions and demands, so getting close to peer performance is what we should shoot for.

This principle can also apply to race-based analyses due to historical discrimination in the United States. Since minority borrowers have historically faced challenges in getting loan financing, they have had fewer opportunities to build wealth. Homeownership rates are then lower, which means they are often paying monthly housing payments in the form of rent payments. Since rent is not reported to credit bureaus like mortgages, these individuals' credit scores would be lower on average, thus making them appear less creditworthy on paper. This then leads to fewer originations for minority individuals and higher denial rates. It is all interrelated.

In certain communities that have experienced higher instances of redlining, peer data is a better indicator of market demands and qualifications. That is not a free pass for an organization to shoot for or settle for the minimum threshold of lending to minority borrowers, it is only a starting point to see if you have heightened redlining risk. It is totally possible for most or all institutions to fall way short of lending based on census demographics, in which case, everyone has a lot of work to do. Institutions that proactively invest in these communities often position themselves as market leaders and uncover growth opportunities others miss.

GEOGRAPHIC DISTRIBUTION ANALYSIS

Geographic distribution is the heart of redlining analysis. If an institution avoids lending in certain geographical areas that it could and should serve, and it is based on the population demographics of those areas, that is essentially redlining. Therefore, a geographical based test is the most critical when it comes to assessing redlining risk.

While we just discussed which data you should shoot for in your reviews, census data is where you start on a geographic distribution test. If 30 percent of the census tracts in your market are majority-minority, you should hopefully be approaching that same percentage in lending activity within those tracts. HMDA data makes this analysis relatively easy, but consumer and commercial loan data can also be used.

We once conducted a fair lending audit for a credit card bank. They had tens of thousands of credit cards issued around the country, and we wanted to see if they were redlining. To do that, we got a list of all cards they issued and the customers' addresses. Our goal was to find the three metro areas with the most volume and perform a redlining analysis.

Not surprisingly, those metro areas were New York, Los Angeles, and Chicago. We then did statistical sampling based on volume and randomly chose our samples of accounts. We ended up reviewing a few hundred accounts from each metro area and geocoded where the cardholders lived. We then pulled the census data to see the percentages of majority-minority census tracts in each metro area and compared the bank's performance with the census data.

What we found was near perfect alignment with the census data. If a metro had 55 percent majority-minority census tracts, our testing found 56 percent of all credit card accounts originated in majority-minority census tracts. Yes, it took a little bit of work gathering all that data, but this was a major credit card issuer that had never really done a geographic distribution analysis of their credit card portfolio. It made them feel good to know they were not redlining in any of those metro areas.

You can do the same analysis for any loan product. All you need is addresses, census data, and a little bit of time.

BORROWER PROFILE ANALYSIS

Borrower profile testing is not as commonly used in a redlining analysis, but we feel it should be. Yes, redlining is very much a geographical based analysis, but spoiler alert: you can lend in high minority areas and still not lend to minority individuals. We have seen it many times.

Let's say you run your HMDA data and do your geographic distribution analysis. You find that 30 percent of your census tracts are majority-minority, and 29 percent of all loans originated in majority-minority census tracts. All is good, right? Not so fast.

Now that you know you are lending proportionately in high minority areas, look and see if you are actually lending to minority individuals in those areas. That is where the borrower profile test comes in.

It is not uncommon to see institutions originate loans in

high-minority areas but primarily to white borrowers. That is why borrower profile testing is a critical component to geographic analysis.

When you look at application rates, denial rates, fallout rates, and origination rates based on race or ethnicity, you are looking at the borrower's profile. You should do the same with redlining to ensure you are originating loans to minority individuals in those higher-minority census tracts.

Bringing It All Together

No single fair lending risk should ever be evaluated in isolation. All risks are interconnected, and redlining is often where they converge. A good compliance or audit professional will look at the whole picture, find the root cause, and then communicate with management suggested corrective actions.

It is important to remember that we in compliance and audit are not risk managers. We are risk identifiers. It is our job to interview staff, use our allocated resources, test files, and cut up and review data to find risks. We then summarize that risk into reports and let management know in review exit meetings and reports what that risk is.

It is then the Board and senior management's responsibility to determine how to respond to that risk. They are the risk managers. We identify and communicate, and they act or do not act.

If you find underwriting risk in denials, holes in branching, or unflattering redlining data, your job is to let the executive team know. They can either accept the risk or reallocate resources to reduce or eliminate it.

Key Takeaways

- Redlining is a geographic-based fair lending risk that often reflects failures across multiple loan lifecycle stages.

- Any fair lending risk can contribute to redlining if left unaddressed.

- Branch locations, marketing, product offerings, staffing, and community engagement all play critical roles.

- HMDA data is the strongest tool for identifying redlining risk.

- Census and peer data should be used together, with context guiding interpretation.

- Geographic distribution and borrower profile tests should be analyzed together.

- Compliance and audit identify risk; management determines how to respond.

CHAPTER ELEVEN

Rolling With the Changes

As the old saying goes, the only constant in this world is change. Regulatory compliance is no different. Some changes are minor footnotes, while others are sweeping and affect nearly everything. The goal of this final chapter is not to cover every possible change, but to talk about different areas of change so you can better prepare for the future.

For the most part, changes in fair lending are slow, but when they happen, they are massive. Redlining, for example, was made illegal in 1968 with the Fair Housing Act. Industry and legal experts argue it was made illegal shortly after the Civil War with a constitutional amendment, but the point remains that the Fair Housing Act represented a major regulatory change affecting fair lending.

Up until 1974, a wife could not obtain a loan without her husband signing for it. That is not that long ago when you think about it. Tory's mom started her own salon business in the early 1960s, and the idea that his dad had to sign for her is mind boggling. The Equal Credit Opportunity Act made discrimination based on sex illegal, and over time, additional prohibited basis factors were added. That was another sweeping regulatory change.

In 1977, the Community Reinvestment Act changed the lending industry yet again with regulatory guidance designed to combat redlining. It remained largely unchanged until 1995 when lawmakers saw a need to update the law. However, it has remained relatively untouched since that time. What was the world like in 1995? Significantly different than it is today. The internet was still in its infancy, and depositing a check by taking a picture with your phone seemed like science fiction because smart phones and watches were still science fiction.

Our world continues to change, and the rules, regulations, and laws need to change with it. That means we must be prepared to adapt as changes occur. This chapter will touch on some super fun topics like politics, but the goal is not to influence your political beliefs. Rather, it is to illustrate how the political landscape impacts how we do business. Regardless of whether we agree or disagree, we still must follow the rules in place at the time.

We will also discuss changes within your own organization. How does growth impact your fair lending program? How do mergers and acquisitions, expansion into new markets, or the introduction of new products affect your fair lending risk?

Let's start with what is hopefully a less controversial topic – the environment.

ENVIRONMENTAL CHANGE

In the not-too-distant past, Tory had the opportunity to host a panel on bluelining at the national fair lending colloquium. You are probably asking the same question that he did when he was first invited to moderate the panel: what is bluelining?

In our own words, bluelining is restricting financial products and services based on geographies that have experienced negative impacts from climate change. Before you ask, yes, there is a significant crossover with redlining.

When thinking about bluelining, hurricanes in Florida are one of the easiest examples to illustrate. Florida is threatened by hurricanes nearly every year. This climate risk causes tremendous damage, which in turn makes insurance difficult to obtain and very expensive. Insurance companies are not in the business of losing money, so when they do lose money, they raise rates. When they lose money frequently, they raise rates frequently, and those costs impact everyone, even those who do not live in those areas.

Hurricane insurance has become extremely expensive in certain regions. If consumers cannot afford or obtain insurance, they also cannot obtain loans and therefore cannot purchase homes. Many areas affected by bluelining due to climate impacts are also high-minority areas that have historically experienced redlining. This is where the two risks intersect.

This is not just limited to hurricanes though. We see similar issues in areas prone to landslides, wildfires, floods, and drought. Regions stripped of natural resources, such as trees, may be more susceptible to flooding and landslides. Increased heat leads to drought and forest fires, prompting many financial institutions to exit these areas altogether. Now, borrowers in these communities are then forced to contend with the lingering effects of redlining while also facing climate change and bluelining.

Bluelining is not yet an official regulatory term. Regulatory agencies have not formally adopted it in examinations, and we are not aware of any enforcement cases specifically citing bluelining. Nonetheless, it remains a real risk, including from a safety and soundness perspective.

POLITICAL CHANGE

If there is one topic you should bring up at the holiday table with your family, it is politics. These discussions always end in spirited and quiet roundtable debates that warm holiday hearts and make people question why they do not get together more often as a family. If you had to go back and reread that again, congratulations, you are still awake. Okay, maybe the world does not quite work that way, but the political environment directly impacts us in our day-to-day lives. The topic cannot just be ignored like cranberry sauce at Thanksgiving dinner. Political decisions influence the laws and regulations we manage within our institutions, so we must address them.

If you have never attended a compliance, banking, or fair lending conference, advocate to go. These are eye-opening events and provide valuable insight into the changing regulatory landscape. If you are reading this book, there is a good chance you received it personally from one of us at a conference. If that is the case, thank you for making it to the end and committing yourself to learn.

Nearly every conference discusses one recurring concept more than any other: "The Pendulum Swing." As the political climate changes every two years with elections, and control of our government changes hands, that pendulum swings back and forth. It makes our jobs increasingly difficult, but you could say it also keeps us relevant.

Generally speaking, one political party favors increased regulatory oversight and stronger consumer protection, which results in more regulatory requirements for financial institutions. The other party typically favors reduced oversight and freer markets, leading to fewer regulatory requirements. There are positives and negatives to both approaches.

It does not matter which camp you fall into from your political views because you must deal with the fallout either way.

The more control one political party has in government, the further we see the pendulum swing in one direction.

Eventually, we know that party will lose control, and then we see the pendulum swing way back the other direction. Some wise individuals once said recently at a conference that it is time to stop the pendulum. Wow, what a profound thought that is. Regulatory consistency across political administrations? Well, that is unlikely to happen, so let's get back to the task at hand.

The overarching point to this is that you should always strive to build a CMS and fair lending program that withstands the swinging pendulum. Let's use a recent example: disparate impact.

Disparate impact occurs when an institution's policies, procedures, or practices have a disproportionate negative effect on a prohibited basis group, even if there is no intent to discriminate. This can include higher pricing in minority areas, stricter underwriting criteria for minority borrowers, or only offering government-guaranteed loans in majority-minority census tracts while offering lower cost conventional loans in white neighborhoods.

Each political administration can choose to enforce disparate impact or not enforce it, but the risk itself does not change. If one political party is less likely to enforce disparate impact, does that mean the risk goes away? Of course not. It is still in the law, and there are more parties interested in it than just your federal regulator.

In 2025, the executive branch sought to stop its enforcement and remove disparate impact from examination manuals and the regulation itself. That same year, several states brought disparate impact cases involving home loans, student lending, and credit cards. While the federal government was taking a step back on disparate impact, state governments were stepping right up to fill the gap.

Private companies and non-profits can also be gatekeepers of financial institution performance, and they can bring private lawsuits against lenders citing disparate impact liability. Just because the current federal government administration does not make a particular part of a law or regulation a priority does not mean the risk is removed.

Another concept frequently discussed at conferences is the look-back period, or how far regulators can review past data when pursuing enforcement actions. We know that some federal agencies will go back three years in their look-back period, and the Department of Justice, who handles most redlining cases, will go back as far as five years. What does that mean for you?

Suppose we are one year into an administration that has made it clear they are not going to pursue fair lending or redlining cases. Your executive team decides to scale back on reviews, personnel, software, and ultimately resources to lend in high-minority areas. For the next three years, you watch your application rates and origination rates decline in high-minority areas. Maybe denials start to increase to minority borrowers, and all along new branches are going up in white neighborhoods and form a nice circle around the high-minority areas. Then, seemingly out of nowhere but also 100% predictable, we have an election. The other party takes over, and that pendulum swings back. Hard.

The new federal government will look back at your performance in the past five years, well beyond the past three where your organization decided to make major changes in resource allocation, and your numbers are terrible. You are now multiple times behind census and peer data performance. Your organization is not devoting any resources to these high-risk areas, you are not conducting any reviews, have no software tools, and no CMS set up to identify the problems, let alone fix them. These are the organizations that are on the high probability list of becoming the next redlining cases.

While wanting to stop the pendulum is a wonderful thought, it is not likely. However, we can build a program and CMS that can withstand any pendulum swing, any regulatory change, and any new political climate. If the current administration is not prioritizing something you know the next one might, do not cut the program and rebuild when the new administration comes in. Keep things going, and you will be ready for the next change. Build when others tear down and be ready, even if today you are not required to be.

ORGANIZATIONAL CHANGE

While external factors like environmental and political change affect fair lending risk, internal organizational changes can be just as impactful.

Tory has taught at the Graduate School of Banking in Colorado for many years and teaches a class on growth. One phrase he uses in every class is simple but powerful: Act Your Asset Size!

What does that really mean? Well, as organizations grow, their programs need to grow with them. We have seen many organizations see significant growth in the lending department, and this fuels a lot of new revenue. Loan growth leads to more interest income, origination fees, and overall revenue. It is awesome. But as much fun it is to see all that money come in, it comes at a price. Yes, financial institutions are good at adding lending staff to fuel that growth and maybe even executive oversight, but who gets left behind?

Support staff like accounting, human resources, compliance, and audit. These areas are viewed as cost centers, yet often their workloads increase dramatically during periods of growth without any corresponding increases in resources to handle it.

As former examiners, we have seen many organizations see massive growth, only to leave the support teams running on fumes. It is not uncommon to see organizations triple in size while expecting the same compliance and audit staff to support them. Hence the phrase: Act Your Asset Size. If you are a bank that went from 10 branches to 30 in 3 years, how has your compliance, audit, and fair lending resources increased to support that growth?

Growth typically occurs in two ways: organically or through mergers and acquisitions (M&As).

Organic growth is when you grow as a company or organization by adding resources and bringing in new customers. This may be opening new branches, offering online or mobile services, and increasing your geographic footprint. It typically happens slowly over time, but it can be deliberate and fueled by capital and earnings to increase its speed with intention. Either way, organic growth eventually comes with additional support resources needed because the slower growth is easier to handle. However, if you do see a rapid increase in lending, the need for support and fair lending resources often becomes an emergency.

M&As are a different animal entirely as an organization can literally double overnight. When two organizations become one, you instantly are much larger than when you started. This creates a lot of positives. You now have resources you did not once have. Perhaps you have better technology, a larger footprint, and access into new markets. These can be positives, but there are negatives you must also navigate.

If the two merging organizations have different cultures, that can create a host of issues. If you have two totally different software platforms, it makes it harder to manage programs. Different philosophies on lending or policies and procedures that do not line up may mean that your entire CMS may need to be altered. In the CMS chapter, we discussed the importance of building up a strong CMS, and already in this chapter we foot stomped having a CMS that will weather the political storm, and now you may need to rebuild it from the ground up.

New Products
and Market Expansion

Introducing new products and services also changes fair lending risk. Any new product requires revisiting the entire loan lifecycle to ensure risks are identified and mitigated, and you might need to enhance your CMS to support the product. All of these can be positives of a healthy and growing institution, but we need to get back to basics when it comes to fair lending to make sure the program is ready.

When you decide to get out of your comfort zone and expand into the community or state next door, new fair lending risks can emerge. The best example is redlining risk.

Time and again we have seen institutions expand towards a new metro area. They do it slowly and over a period of years, but they start with the suburbs. They open branches away from the downtown areas, and they expand around but not in the metro area. They fail to realize that they are slowly creating a donut around the downtown high-minority areas, and before they know it, they have nine branches on a minority map that look like a textbook example in a redlining case.

We can see that same issue in M&As. If you are acquiring a new institution, you need to review the branch footprint and insert all branches (new and current) together to see the full picture. You inherit all the problems from the institution you are buying, so know those issues beforehand.

We know that compliance, audit, and fair lending professionals are not always invited to the table when it comes to discussions on growth. If you are an executive reading this book, we hope you now see the value of having those trusted risk identifiers in the discussion early. If you are a compliance or audit professional often left out of the discussion, open up dialog into the importance of your participation. That does not mean you need to be at every meeting, but it is important to have an idea of plans and being able to anticipate risks can save a lot of headaches down the road.

KEY TAKEAWAYS

- Environmental, political, and organizational changes all impact fair lending risk.

- Regulatory change is constant, and so your fair lending program must be built to adapt to pendulum swings.

- Scaling back fair lending efforts during low-enforcement periods increases future risk.

- Organizational growth should correspond with growth in compliance and audit resources – Act Your Asset Size!

Conclusion

Fair lending does not have to be difficult. There are basic concepts that you should know, and hopefully after reading this book, you have a much better understanding of those concepts.

You do not have to go alone. Seek help. Get further educated in fair lending. Do not let one short book be everything you know on the topic. Check out our fair lending school if you are looking for that in-depth training – www.tcuniversity.us. Our Fair Lending School and certification course goes much further in-depth than we ever can in a book.

Look for consultants that know the topic and can help you identify risk. Build those relationships with trusted third parties that can steer you in the right direction.

Seek out software solutions. There is no magic number of HMDA lines when you should start considering software. However, if you are crossing the 400-500 lines threshold, you need to know what your data says, whether you get your own software or pay to have someone tell you what your data says.

Final Takeaway

Fair lending is an open book test. You get to literally look up the answers before the regulators show up. Go through the lifecycle risks and find out where you stand. Ignorance is never an excuse.

However, if you find issues, ACT! The only thing worse than having major fair lending issues and not knowing about it, is knowing and doing nothing. We start seeing formal enforcement actions from federal regulators when they must force an institution to change. If you identify your own issues and start putting effective corrective action in place, you will be viewed in a much more positive and collaborative light in the regulator's eyes during the next examination. They may still criticize you and offer recommendations on how to improve, but they also know you are on the right track and do not have to force your hand. If you have done nothing to fix issues, it is likely time to buckle up because it is going to be an uncomfortable ride.

Be proactive.

About the Authors

Tory Haggerty is a multiple best-selling author. He is a nationwide speaker on fair lending, training thousands of bankers, lenders, and compliance professionals across the US in a nearly 20-year career. Tory has earned three college degrees including an MBA, five industry certifications, and is a commissioned examiner with the FDIC. He is an alumnus and current instructor at the Graduate School of Banking – Colorado. In 2025, his TEDx Talk – *Fair lending for the new generation* has garnered more than 2.5 million views, making it one of the most viewed TEDx talks of all time. In 2020, Tory retired as captain in the United States Air Force.

Jonathan Gilmor is a distinguished compliance professional who has worked on more than one hundred regulatory compliance and audit engagements. Jon earned a bachelor's degree in business administration with a focus in finance, graduating as class valedictorian. He has earned multiple industry certifications and is a commissioned examiner with the FDIC. Prior to his consulting role, Jon served as a regulatory liaison for a 100-billion-dollar financial institution.